John Lawson Stoddard

Red-Letter Days Abroad

John Lawson Stoddard

Red-Letter Days Abroad

ISBN/EAN: 9783744692533

Printed in Europe, USA, Canada, Australia, Japan

Cover: Foto ©ninafisch / pixelio.de

More available books at **www.hansebooks.com**

RED-LETTER DAYS ABROAD

BY

JOHN L. STODDARD

𝔚𝔦𝔱𝔥 𝔍𝔩𝔩𝔲𝔰𝔱𝔯𝔞𝔱𝔦𝔬𝔫𝔰

BOSTON

JAMES R. OSGOOD AND COMPANY

1884

UNIVERSITY PRESS:

JOHN WILSON AND SON, CAMBRIDGE.

TO MY FRIEND,

HERR MESMER,

Of Baden-Baden, Germany,

BENEATH WHOSE HOSPITABLE ROOF MANY OF THESE DESCRIPTIONS HAVE
BEEN WRITTEN DURING INTERVALS OF REPOSE FROM TRAVEL,
AND WITH WHOM THUS ARE DELIGHTFULLY
ASSOCIATED MY

RED-LETTER DAYS ABROAD.

CONTENTS.

———◆———

LIST OF ILLUSTRATIONS.

———◦———

TRAVEL
IN SUNNY SPAIN

RED-LETTER DAYS ABROAD.

TRAVELS IN SUNNY SPAIN.

NOT many years ago, a tour in Spain was regarded as a dangerous enterprise. Even the Spaniards themselves, when about to travel in their own country, first, as a matter of course, sent for a priest to absolve their sins, a doctor to give them medicine, and a lawyer to make their wills. Within a few years, however, travelling conveniences have so far improved, that priest, physician, and advocate are now no longer deemed so indispensable for a Spanish journey as a full purse and a reliable guide-book. And yet, unfortunately, almost all European travellers fail to visit Spain. But they lose thereby a country scarcely to be surpassed in interest by any on the globe. Do we desire sublime and varied scenery? It is there spread broadcast, skirted by the classic Mediterranean and canopied by a sky of incomparable depth and beauty. For beneath its azure dome not only bloom the olive, the pomegranate, the orange and the palm; but there, in vivid contrast to these, are rugged mountains and savage, solitary plains, noble and majestic even in their severity. Are we in quest of art? Many of the grandest cathedrals in the world rear in Spain their vast proportions; while her famous picture-gallery at Madrid is the equal of any in Italy, and the superior of all the rest in Europe. Finally, do we look for historic interest? Then surely we shall not be disappointed here; for Spain is a country which speaks to us of the successive dominion of many powerful races, each of which has left behind it indestructible evidences of its sway.

Thus ruins dating back to the Roman, Goth, Moor, and Christian greet us at every turn, fanned by the perfumed breath of orange-trees, or shaded by the drooping fringes of the palm. For let us remember that from Spain Roman emperors have arisen, to wear the Imperial Purple of the world; in Spain the gifted Moors ruled

THE CITY OF TOLEDO.

for seven centuries in splendor; while Spain it was that discovered America, and held for years in her controlling hands the destinies of the two hemispheres!

In imagination let us enter this fascinating and romantic land of Spain, seeing first before us the far-famed city of Toledo. It is one of the most interesting places in all Spain, and, with the exception of Jerusalem, the most picturesquely located city in the world. Viewed from near or far, the situation of Toledo is indeed magnificent: enthroned upon a rocky bluff twenty-four hundred feet above the sea. At its base the river Tagus, surging and boiling through a chasm in the granite hills, girdles the city almost completely, leaving only one avenue of approach on the land side, which is itself defended by old Moorish walls and towers. Moreover, like the throne of Hercules, the mythical founder of the place, the hill on which Toledo stands rises almost perpendicularly from the waves, completely terraced with old houses, churches, palaces and convents, until the summit is crowned by the enormous, orange-colored citadel of the Alcazar, frowning for miles over the surrounding plain.

What wonder that with such a situation Toledo has been besieged more than a score of times? What marvel that every conqueror who beholds it covets and resolves to have it? For what a history has this gloomy, castle-crowned city! Founded long before the Christian era by the Phœnicians, it was afterward the resort of the Jews, who fled hither after the destruction of Jerusalem, only to find this city also ruled by the all-conquering Romans. Then came the Goths, who drove the Romans out of Spain, as they had previously crushed Rome in Italy. To these again succeeded the Moors, who, perched like eagles on these rocky heights, bade defiance to their foes for centuries. But finally they too were driven forth by another set of conquerors; namely, the Christians, who having gained possession of these historic cliffs have ever since retained them.

The various means of approach to this old Spanish town consist of a number of picturesque bridges, which one after the other in the course of centuries have flung across the Tagus their gigantic forms. One of these was erected more than seven hundred years ago, to replace a Moorish structure; and connected with its ponderous old arch is an odd story of womanly stratagem. It seems that the architect discovered, when too late, that his work was not strong enough, and must inevitably fall beneath a heavy burden. To his wife alone he whispered in despair his unhappy secret. "All is not lost," exclaimed this lady of Toledo; "trust but to me, and you can still retrieve yourself." Accordingly that very night she caused the bridge to be set on fire, and by burning down the entire structure saved her husband's reputation; for, profiting by his former error, he made in the construction of this arch no such fault.

Less ancient than this, but wonderfully graceful, is the bridge of Alcantara, revealed to us in the illustration, spanning the glittering Tagus in a single arch. Near this point formerly lived that lovely girl whose charms were destined to overthrow the Gothic empire in Spain. The last of the Gothic kings who sat upon the throne of Toledo was Roderick, the shameless traitor to his friend, the base betrayer of the innocent maiden intrusted to his care. But, solicited by the father of the injured girl, on came the Moors in their career of conquest; to meet whom Roderick went forth in a chariot of ivory, and dressed in gold and purple, but was destined, despite all this magnificence, to encounter ignominious defeat and death on the banks of Guadalquivir, where the fate of the Goths in Spain was sealed, and their power smitten to the earth by the resistless Moors.

If you are not tired of Toledo tales, let me tell you another. Just beyond this bridge is a little church called "Christ of the Valley." Within it is a crucifix, decorated, as usual in Spain, with real hair. This has a most singular history. The figure of Christ, which is of life size, has only one hand nailed to the cross; the other is stretched out toward the spectator. A poor peasant girl once made her lover swear that he would marry her if she accepted his caresses. The lover broke his oath and deserted her; whereupon the unhappy girl came to this church and called upon the crucified one to come to her rescue, and prove to the world her promise of marriage. He is said to have done so; for before the breathless spectators the hand of Christ detached itself from the cross, and on the silent air were heard the solemn words, "*I am the witness!*" An artist would consider this story a fine theme for a poem or a painting. The more practical answer would be that few breach-of-promise suits are as well sustained.

Meantime you have doubtless noticed that beyond the portcullis and the tower, which mark the two extremities of the bridge, the road winds gradually around the hill, like an Alpine pass, leading to yonder Alcazar, — that stronghold of so many conquerors, around whose walls the angry flood of war has often dashed its crimson waves. This was once so magnificent, alike in decoration and dimensions, that Charles V., when he first entered it, exclaimed : " To-day I feel as never before that I am an Emperor and a King ! " But

GATEWAY OF THE SUN.

now the ravages of time and man have so defaced its galleries and gorgeous halls, that the once proud Alcazar of Toledo is nothing but a shell of granite, looking profoundly sad and desolate above the lonely river. Only its indestructible walls remain to tell us that it was once for centuries the palatial fortress of successive rulers. But crossing now this handsome bridge, let us approach one of the massive Portals of Toledo, the Gateway of the Sun, — a splendid symbol of its ancient glory. Such an entrance gate as this reminds us that formerly this city was the pride of Spain, as famous in the world as Constantinople or Damascus. The favorite city of the exiled Jew, the stronghold of the Goth, the metropolis of the Moor, and the capital of the Christian, it still bears the seal of grandeur in its walls and towers. Yet, when I passed beneath this Moorish arch, although it was the hour of noon, it appeared wellnigh as tranquil and deserted as we here behold it. The grass was growing in the pavement. Few people were visible. The sleep of a thousand years seemed to have

fallen upon the inhabitants, from which they will probably n e v e r wake to resume the old life of the ninth century. *Ilium fuit!* The glory of Toledo has departed.

We realize this emphatically when, passing on beneath this gate, we enter a characteristic Toledo street. Not surely a place for rapid driving! The rough pavement almost dislocates our joints as we jolt over it. Nor is it an agreeable place for a promenade. There are those who date the birth of their corns to a walk in

A SPANISH STREET.

this old Spanish town! Once in our walks through this city of the past we heard a rumbling like distant thunder, which gradually came nearer and nearer, startling us by its contrast to the usual tomb-like stillness of the place. The cause was soon apparent. It was the hotel omnibus; one of the few vehicles of which Toledo can boast. We were in one of the comparatively broad streets, yet had to step into a doorway to avoid being crushed by the passing wheels, which almost grazed the houses in their course.

Tradition says that in the days of the Christian conquest, when that famous Spanish chieftain, the Cid, was riding through one of these Toledan streets, his horse suddenly fell on its knees. In these ungodly times, when our horses try thus to appear devotional, we force them to get up and go on; and if they refuse, we suspect them of having the blind staggers. Not so in the time of the Cid. When *his* old mare knelt down, all knew that she was influenced by some religious motive. Accordingly they pulled down a wall before which she was kneeling, and as the stones fell, a stream of light poured forth. Was it a candle? Perish the thought! A crucifix was discovered there, which had been hidden by the Goths centuries before, when the Moors took the city. The altar lamp was still burning miraculously, and the Cid's devout horse was of course regarded as inspired. We saw the crucifix and the lamp. Upon the former was a figure of Christ with real hair reaching nearly to the waist. The lamp still burns. · It is said that an irreverent American upon hearing this story inquired: "Has that 'ere lamp been burning for a thousand years?" "Si, Señor, for one towsand years." Murmuring "One thousand years," the American bent over it and suddenly gave a tremendous puff. Horrors! The lamp was extinguished! "There," exclaimed the representative of the stars and stripes, "the plaguy thing is out now anyway!"

On both sides of us, as we ride along, rise high and massive houses, severe and melancholy in appearance, solid as citadels, and pierced with occasional grated windows. We realize that we are in the very heart of Northern Spain. The dwellings are not open as in the southern towns of Andalusia. No charming courtyards reveal their flowers and fountains behind trellises of open iron-work. On the contrary the gateways seem almost like the portals of a fortress, flanked as they are by columns of granite, while their heavy oaken doors are studded with enormous iron nails. Two ponderous iron knockers hang upon these doors; one to be used by pedestrians, the other, much higher, to be struck by horsemen. Everything seems sombre, stern and mysterious. This is indeed a city of the past,— almost as sad and silent as a tomb. I can recall no town so utterly devoid of modern characteristics, so hopelessly sunk in the ruins of past grandeur. It is the ghost of a departed glory.

Yet Spain is probably richer in cathedrals than any other country in the world; and one of the grandest of them all is at Toledo. The

A TOLEDEAN HOUSE.

Virgin Mary is said to have a special liking for it; and if this be true, she certainly possesses excellent taste. She has even paid it frequent visits, I am told; and once actually descended for the special purpose of putting a new robe on St. Ildefonso, one of its archbishops. This scene is constantly represented in sculpture and painting in all parts of the cathedral, and, to preclude all doubt about it, the very stone is shown on which the Virgin alighted. Encased in red marble, it is surrounded by a railing, and over it is the following inscription: "We will worship in the place where her feet have stood."

There are several statues of the Virgin in this Toledo cathedral, each of which possesses a gorgeous toilette. One especially has a mantle for gala days, with seventy-eight thousand pearls embroidered on it! Not content with that, she wears, moreover, a great many diamonds, rubies, and emeralds.

Her crown alone cost more than twenty-five thousand dollars, and her bracelets are valued at ten thousand. These are presents of

kings and queens, popes, archbishops, and private ladies of wealth.
Nor is this strange; for the Virgin ranks as a queen, in Spain, and
always wears the royal crown.　To one particular statue of Mary, near
Madrid, the queens of Spain have for years given their wedding
dresses.　She wears them in processions, and has several trunks
filled with them.　How few virgins are so fortunate!

It is also a fact that the greatest ladies of the kingdom take charge
of the wardrobe, altars, and decorations of the Virgin, much as the
ancients did in regard to the statues of Diana, Juno, and Venus.
Even the poorest village in Spain has some statue of Mary; and
when rival processions meet, the worshippers of one town have more
than once insulted the rival image of the other, pelting it with stones,
but defending theirs with knife and pistol!

I went to one chapel in this cathedral to see a "genuine portrait" of the Virgin.　Much to my astonishment, I found it to consist of a wooden statue, so darkened by time as to closely resemble a
negress.　It is said to be authentic, and unhappily there is no way of
disproving it.　At all events, it is covered with silver and jewels.

While speaking of this feature of the Toledo cathedral, let me
mention another, which is, indeed, characteristic of all the churches
in Spain.　Hanging on both sides of almost every Spanish altar are
miniature arms, legs, hands, noses, and feet, made of wax, suspended
there in great numbers, as though they were ornaments for a Christmas
tree.　On inquiry, I learned that they all represent *cures* which are
supposed to have been effected by the Virgin's aid.　There is a simplicity about this which is striking.　Instead of the votive tables of
the French churches, which coldly state the unembellished facts of
recovery, we have in Spain the more eloquent testimonials of the wax
figures.　Thus if a lame leg has been cured by the Virgin, the wax
limb is hung up as a triumphant proof of the miracle.

But all this is soon forgotten when we turn away from statues
and relics of Virgin and saints to contemplate the grand proportions
and beautiful architecture of the edifice itself.　After the bright glare
of the Spanish sunlight without, it is a pleasure to find ourselves in
the grateful twilight of the interior.　It is much less dark than the

cathedral of Seville, and its seven hundred and fifty iris-colored windows flood the vast edifice with a marvellously beautiful combination of light and shade.

INTERIOR OF THE TOLEDO CATHEDRAL.

The pavement on which we walk is a variegated marble, and around us are twenty-three fine chapels of different styles and periods. Upon this cathedral, indeed, the greatest artists of Spain labored successively during six centuries. Wonder not then that it excited our enthusiasm. For example, the choir of this church is decorated with probably the most elaborate wood-carvings in the world. It was unfortunately the fashion of Spanish architects to place the choir — that is, the place where the service is chanted — in the very centre of the church; an arrangement which blocks up the great nave, and sadly interferes with the general perspective down the main aisle. But in this case our disappointment at its position is fully compensated by the beauty which it reveals to us on entering. It is a veritable museum of mediæval sculpture in wood. Around a pavement made of large white marble slabs rise on three sides two rows of seats for the priests, one above the other. I have never seen any thing comparable to these sacerdotal chairs, although all Spanish cathedrals are rich in carvings which somewhat resemble them.

The arms, backs, feet, head-pieces, and railings of these seats are most elaborately wrought into sacred, grotesque, mythological, or historic subjects in bas-relief.

The upper row is the work of the celebrated rivals, Berruguete and Philip of Borgona, who, after a bitter contest, undertook their tasks, each determined to excel the other. One carved the seats on one side of the choir, the other the opposite ones. It is, indeed, difficult to say who deserves the palm; for, as there was contention between the sculptors, so there will always be disagreement in the opinions of spectators. Moreover, these seats are separated by beautiful jasper pillars, with alabaster basements and capitals; and over them all extends a series of alabaster medallions, with figures of the saints and patriarchs in relief.

Just beyond this magnificent choir are the high chapel and altar, which produce a most imposing effect. In imagination linger with me for a moment here. The splendid sacerdotal chairs are behind us. We are standing within a chapel fifty-six feet long and fifty wide, while the sculptured, gilded, and painted roof, one hundred and sixteen feet above us, looks like a miniature sky. The marble piers which support this are decorated with a veritable population of statues, representing kings, bishops, saints, and angels with outspread wings. Before us, broad steps of jasper and colored marble lead up to the high altar, behind which rises in grandeur the most imposing object in the whole cathedral.   This is the *retablo*, or altar-screen, — the work of twenty-seven artists, and the pride of Toledo.   You can form some idea of this when I tell you that it rises from the pavement to the very roof, and is therefore one hundred and sixteen feet high. It is. divided into five stories, separated by elaborately wrought columns, the material being wood, richly painted, carved, and gilded. These stories are profusely ornamented with statuettes, columns, colossal figures, arabesques, and filigree work, of whose combined effect no description can give an adequate idea; for all these are painted and gilded with extraordinary richness.

We had left this splendid work of the mediæval artists, and found ourselves in one of the side aisles of the cathedral.   As these approach the head of the Latin cross which forms the ground plan of this grand edifice, they wind about the high altar with a beautiful curve, which is charming from its grace, and awe-inspiring from its lofty and majestic sweep.   As we entered this curving avenue of pillars, a sight burst upon our view which I can never forget, and which irresistibly silenced our voices into whispers, and for a moment held us spell-bound where we stood.   The lofty roof of the cathedral seemed to have opened, and there, in the glory of ten thousand sunbeams, we saw a multitude of angels, cherubs, saints, and apostles, descending from the opened skies.   For an instant the illusion was as perfect as if we were witnessing a celestial vision.

Nor was this effect strange.   Directly behind the grand *retablo*, which I have described, there is really a circular opening in the ceiling through which the light freely enters.   Around and within this, as far as the eye can reach, is a multitude of marble figures, whose appearance thus is that of saints and angels descending on the clouds of heaven.   In no other cathedral of the world have I ever seen such a design, and I can recall few more effective.   Perhaps at some other time the impression would have been different.   But we beheld it shortly before sunset, when the long naves were darkening in the twilight and the storied windows of the cathedral were glowing like tablets of rubies and emeralds.   At such an hour this lofty, statue-crowned aperture, through which the rays of sunset poured like a noiseless cataract of gold, seemed like the wondrous revelation of another world.

But, interesting as Toledo is from an historical or artistic point of view, candor compels me to confess that, so far as *material comforts* are concerned, Toledo is not a place to satisfy the epicure or pleasure-seeker. Once, for example, wearied by continued sight-seeing and conscious of an aching void which naught but food could fill, we made our way to that establishment which in Toledo is called by courtesy a hotel. In its courtyard were an unusual number of filthy, blear-eyed beggars, whose smell, appearance and whinings were enough to turn one's stomach. Two waiters, gossiping with a girl in the hall, received my order for dinner with perfect indifference, and smoked cigarettes all the time I was talking. At the end of half an hour's waiting I went in search of them again. I found them still smoking, but having really gotten so far as to set the table. Using the choicest Castilian I could muster, I bade them hurry, as we wished to catch the train for Madrid. With the most indifferent air they removed their cigarettes from their mouths long enough to say "Immediately." At the end of another half-hour I entered the dining-hall, ready to wreak vengeance on anything or anybody I could find. Fortunately the meal was at last ready. The waiters, however, continued smoking all the time they served it; and the sight of their tobacco-stained, jaundiced-looking fingers was not particularly appetizing. Moreover, at the other end of the table was a wedding party. The guests were most repulsively uproarious. All the men were smoking, guzzling wine, and joking coarsely with the bride and her friends. One female (I can hardly call her anything else) was slapping men familiarly on the shoulders and rocking about in her chair, as if she were intoxicated. Having declined a certain dish, the bridegroom insisted that she should take some,—and so strenuously, indeed, that he rose from his seat, made the circuit of the table with a piece of greasy meat upon a fork, and tried to force it into the woman's mouth. Failing in this, he actually *rubbed the meat over her face* amid the yells of the company. In the midst of such pleasing surroundings we took our Toledo dinner!

I will not describe the dishes of this repast. Indeed I could not. They were indescribable. The bread was so hard that, having attempted several times in vain to break it, I decided to take my loaf home as a paper-weight. The wine tasted like stale vinegar. There was no butter. That is a rarity everywhere in Spain, and when one does get it, he might as well eat French pomade. As for the meat,— it fully justified the Spanish proverb: " God sends good meat to Spain, but the devil cooks it."

While we were worrying down fragments of this memorable meal, I noticed upon the table-cloth near my plate a black dot,— I mean blacker than the rest of the cloth, for all of it was dirty. I put my hand out to remove it, when to my surprise it leaped into my plate! I said nothing to my suffering companions, but sat for some time musing over the question, why Noah ever admitted a pair of fleas into the ark. Doubtless they took up less room than most of the animals, and proved very lively companions. But oh, Father Noah, if you only could have spared them, your loss would have been for us travellers a blessed gain; for at the present time the traveller must come to Spain expecting not to eat, but to be eaten. As a rule, Spanish cooking is detestable. Of course in the best hotels (when kept by French landlords) one can fare quite well. But once leave the large cities and try small towns like Toledo and Burgos, and, unless you resort to oranges, you will well-nigh perish from hunger. If you ask for bread, you will receive (almost literally) a stone. The ruling principle of Spanish cookery is stewing, for from a scarcity of fuel roasting is almost unknown. Sauces are full of garlic and oil. Even the celebrated Spanish chocolate was pronounced by every one of us to be wretched stuff, though there are some who extol its virtues to the skies. Cooking is surely not the brilliant feature of Spain, and has hardly improved since the days of Don Quixote; while its smaller hotels are as devoid of comfort and as full of animals as Noah's ark ever could have been.

But we shall speedily forget such minor miseries as these, if now we take a more extensive view from one of the battlements of Toledo. From this we look directly down upon the stern and melancholy Tagus, whose surface we again behold reflecting the arches of that massive bridge gray with the mists of seven centuries. If there be a river in the world which has apparently failed to fulfil its mission, it is the one on which we look. Designed by Nature to be the grand highway of Spain, it nevertheless flows on quite solitary and unused for many hundred miles. It might be made navigable to the sea, and thus connect interior Spain with Lisbon and the Atlantic. Yet for a great extent its waves are furrowed by no white winged fleets ; its waters reflect castles and dungeons instead of ports and warehouses, and scarcely even a village rises from its banks. No commerce finds a channel here, and although its sands are reported to be in reality, as they are in appearance, golden, this

THE MELANCHOLY TAGUS.

misused, melancholy Tagus flows idly on through plains which now lie barren and untilled, but which the magic wand of the Moor once made to blossom like a garden. Its barren banks remind us of the Spanish proverb : " The lark which would traverse this country must bring its own grain." I can never forget the view which greeted us as we left Toledo on the edge of evening. Its mighty walls and towers rose grandly above us, isolated from the rest of the world by the solitude of their surroundings, and standing out against the evening sky as solemn and mysterious as a vision of the past. At last the setting sun turned one by one the ripples of this river to a glittering pavement. Through the ruined towers it flung the ruddy glow of a conflagration, tingeing them with that soft vermilion blush which only the southern sun can bestow upon the buildings of the past. In that golden twilight the harsh outlines of its battlements grew soft and mellow, until the many scars inflicted there by time and man were all concealed; while glittering in the saffron west, the grand Alcazar looked like a vast sarcophagus of gold, in which the glory of dead empires lay entombed.

But from Toledo let us now hasten southward into the district of Andalusia, to find upon its very threshold the famous city Cordova, — a place so thronged with impressive memories that I hardly know where to begin in my description. More than two thousand years ago it was a famous Roman city; but its especial glory dates from the conquest of the Moors. With their advent so brilliant an era of prosperity was ushered in that it received the name of the "Athens of the West." Indeed, the wealth, luxury and refinement of Cordova under the Moors reads like an Eastern tale. In the tenth century, when all Christian Europe was sunk in the depths of ignorance, witchcraft and semi-barbarism, Cordova possessed nearly a million inhabitants. Within these walls were then six hundred mosques, fifty hospitals, nine hundred baths, six hundred inns, eight hundred schools, and a library of six hundred thousand volumes! And that, too, when four hundred years later the royal library of France consisted of only nine hundred volumes!

Let us recall just here the testimony of the great scientist and philosopher, Humboldt, than whom we could desire no higher authority. "The Arabs," he says, "have enlarged our views of nature, and enriched science with a great number of new creations. They deserve to be regarded as the veritable founders of physical science, even taking those words in the extended sense which they bear to-day. They may almost be said to have created botany. Chemistry is no less indebted to them. They cultivated geography and geometry with success. Astronomy especially owes to them an extensive development, and they determined the duration of the earth's annual revolution with an exactness which differs but one or two minutes from the most recent calculations."

Meantime, have you noticed this structure before us? It is the ruined tower of Abdurrahman the Great, — the most enlightened of

all the caliphs of Cordova. It once formed part of his almost unrivalled palace, but now serves only as a melancholy symbol of decay. As we look upon it, we remember that it was by this Abdurrahman's order that the streets of Cordova were the first paved in Europe, — admirably

TOWER OF ABDURRAHMAN.

constructed *two hundred years before the first paving stone was laid in Paris.*

Here too, under the Moors, one could walk for miles at night illumined all the way by public lamps, *seven hundred years before the first street-lamp was lit in London;* while by the Moors encyclopedias and scientific treatises were written, when many Christian princes could scarcely read or write. Ah! it was a terrible day for Cordova, and for all Spain, when the high-bred, courteous Moors were driven out of this country which they had ruled so well for centuries. Wealth, learning, art, industry and the charm of

Oriental life went largely with them, and Spain has been unquestionably lower in the scale of prosperity and intelligence ever since.

Nowhere, perhaps, do we realize this more practically than when we look upon a Cordovan wagon, with its clumsy frame and wheels of ill-shaped solid blocks of wood. This is primitive locomotion in-

A CORDOVAN WAGON.

deed. Yet this is only characteristic of the place. To a system of agriculture which, under the Arabs, made of this country the garden of the world, has succeeded a method which uses the root of a tree for a plough, and for a means of transportation the back of a donkey or such a wretched vehicle as this. Indeed, since the expulsion of the Moors the population of Cordova has dwindled from a million to forty thousand. Its nine hundred public baths have disappeared; its six hundred inns have been reduced to two; its skill and industries have vanished; the light of its great universities has been put out; while, to crown all, in Andalusia, where we now are, the country of the gifted Moors, in whose embrace are Cordova, Seville, and Granada, in one of its provinces, out of a population of three hundred and sixty thousand, in this nineteenth century more than three hundred thousand cannot read or write.

Nevertheless, one monument remains in Cordova to attest its ancient glory, unique and without a rival in the world. It is the Moorish Mosque. This alone would well repay a special visit to Spain. In the exterior, however, one can at present discover nothing either Moorish or beautiful; for that has suffered shameful desecration. When the Christians captured the city, they dedicated this building to the Virgin Mary, and sought to "purify" it by defacing its Moorish decorations. Before this mosque, for example, in the time of the Moors, was (and, for that matter, still is) a beautiful court-yard filled with orange-trees and forming a kind of vestibule to the mosque itself. Standing beneath the snowy orange blossoms, the

Moslem saw before him then a façade of nineteen beautiful horse-shoe arches, separated from each other by magnificent columns, and open thus continually between the orange grove on one side and the grand interior on the other. Now, however, these pillars are badly mutilated, and all the arches are walled up save one. Through this remaining

THE MOSQUE OF CORDOVA.

doorway, therefore, let us enter the wondrous Mosque of Cordova. At the first glance we seem to have passed within some sacred grove; for before us is a perfect forest of marble, jasper, porphyry, and alabaster columns. They cross each other at right angles, forming in one direction nineteen and in the other twenty-nine parallel naves, connected by innumerable Moorish arches. We look down the long perspectives and can with difficulty discern their end; for the dimensions of this mosque actually exceed those of St. Peter's at Rome. Think of it ! There are here no less than *one thousand and ninety-six* of these marble columns, *each one of them a monolith* — one single block of polished stone ! Moreover, every one of these has an eventful history. They are the spoils of the temples of the East and West. Some are from the shrines of Carthage ; others are from Rome ; others from Constantinople ; some are from Jerusalem, and on them Jesus may have looked ; while two are from Damascus, and were highly prized by Abdurrahman eleven hundred years ago ! Truly there are memories in the dusky aisles of this marble forest which make the heart beat quickly and the eyes grow dim !

As we walk through this labyrinth of porphyry and jasper, we continually ask ourselves in amazement, "If the impression made upon us *now* by this mosque is awe-inspiring, what would it have been in the days of the Caliphs?" For then four thousand seven hundred gilded lamps flooded it with radiance. The number of these columns was then more than twelve hundred. The ceiling was all of cedar-wood carved to represent overhanging tropical foliage. The floors, too, were covered with Oriental rugs, and in the shadow of these polished shafts knelt hundreds of adoring worshippers.

But this contrast leads me to speak of something which it is difficult even to mention in cool blood while remaining in Cordova, namely, the desecration of this mosque by the Spaniards. Not satisfied with the "purification" which they had effected without, they whitewashed over and totally destroyed the sculptured ceiling of cedarwood, so beautiful as to be worthy of the Alhambra. All the outside aisles were filled up with forty-five cheap and tawdry chapels, thus walling in more than one hundred of these splendid columns ; and sixty more were levelled in the centre of the mosque to make room for an ugly chapel two hundred feet in length, which, placed in this maze of slender monoliths, looks like a hideous tumor, obstructs the view, and exasperates the beholder.

When Charles V., who was himself something of a Vandal, beheld this barbarism, he was indignant with the monks who had effected it, exclaiming, " You have built here what might have been built any-

where, but you have destroyed that which was unique in the world."
But it was then too late for repentance: the irreparable evil had been
done. As I lingered, therefore, in the shadowed aisles of this sculptured grove and breathed the perfumed air of its orange-laden court-
yard, the chanting of the Spanish priests fell strangely on my ear,
and I seemed to be standing beside the tomb of that great Moorish
genius, which has, alas! passed away forever.

But from historic Cordova let us hasten now to fair Seville, the
Paris of Andalusia, the gayest city of all Spain, the home of Figaro
and Don Juan.
Glittering like a
jewel on the
banks of the
Guadalquivir, en-
vironed by or-
ange groves and
palms, and glow-
ing under an ar-
dent sun, it is
almost an Orien-
tal city. Its in-
habitants are
the merriest of

THE CITY OF SEVILLE.

all Spaniards, and, like the Neapolitans, are careless children of
the sun. Many of them seem to live — who can tell how? — on
an orange or a bit of bread, yet always have strength enough left
to thrum a guitar or dance a fandango. They sleep on the steps of
churches, they warm themselves in the sun, and know of heaven
only what they see of it through the smoke of their cigarettes as
they lie on their backs in the cool shade, the very pictures of *dolce
far niente.*

Long before one reaches Seville, he sees in the distance the especial
marvel of the place, — its grand Cathedral. The very spot on which
it stands has been for twenty centuries a place of worship. Venus,

Jesus, Allah, and now Jesus again, have been in turn worshipped here in temple, basilica, mosque and church; but one shrine has given place to another, until now we see before us the noblest cathedral of Spain, and therefore of necessity one of the finest in the world.   Above this, and rising far higher than the intervening build-

THE GIRALDA.

ings, we note the famous Giralda, or bell-tower, built long ago by the Moors, that from its summit the muezzin might call the faithful to prayer, as is done in all the cities of the East to-day.   Let us approach this Giralda, until, from the extremity of a narrow street, we view its entire length rising, as it does, to the height of three hundred and fifty feet. Under the Moors this must have been wonderfully beautiful. Its square walls were then decorated with elegant designs on a background of rose color, fragments of which still remain. Then, too, its summit was surmounted with four enormous golden balls, whose lustre was discernible at a distance of twenty-five miles, and whose value was no less than two hundred and fifty thousand dollars. But these costly ornaments were destroyed by an earthquake in 1395, and now the Giralda is crowned by a colossal female figure in bronze, which, although fourteen feet in height and weighing more than a ton, is nevertheless so nicely balanced that it turns with the slightest breeze. But what do you suppose this statue represents? If you can believe it, *Faith!* Truly a strange subject for a weather-vane, never steadfast, but blown about by every wind! I suspect the architect was a practical joker.

By the way, speaking of the Giralda, it is recorded in the history of this city that, one day early in the Christian era, a precious statue of Venus was being borne through the streets of Seville in a grand procession, much as statues of Jesus and the Virgin Mary are carried there to-day. Two girls recently converted to Christianity would not do it reverence as it passed, and consequently were at once put to death by the angry multitude. These martyred maidens are now the the patron saints of Seville. One sees their pictures everywhere. Tradition says that in 1504, during a terrific thunder-storm, the Devil tried to blow over the cathedral bell-tower in Seville, but that these saints were too much for him. They held it up with their fair hands, and all that his Satanic Majesty could do was to blow and be — disappointed. This miracle is represented in painting or sculpture in every church of Seville, and even Murillo has consecrated to the breezy story one of his finest paintings.

In the month of May we had in Seville an atmosphere of midsummer, yet the air was not oppressive with heat. The top of the carriage shielded us from the burning rays of the sun, and thus protected we were in perfect comfort. Moreover, the streets are narrow, and are therefore usually shaded by the adjoining walls.

As we ride along, we notice that all the buildings are made of white stone; that awnings screen the doors and windows of the

STREET IN SEVILLE.

shops; that the streets are clean and paved with large flag-stones, and that all the ladies are decorated with flowers. Spanish girls, indeed, always have a rose or a carnation among their dark locks, arranged with inimitable grace. To the right and left we look in through gates of prettily wrought iron, and see charming court-yards, paved with marble and surrounded by walls of colored tiles. In these we note admiringly orange and lemon trees, and beautiful flowers and shrubs. Sometimes tall evergreens, planted at each corner of the court, are bent over towards each other until their four tops meet to form a pretty arbor, under which the family take breakfast and tea. In these Sevillian court-yards also may be heard in the evening the piano, the guitar and the Spanish song, to which the murmur of a fountain adds a gentle accompaniment. Now a sudden turn in the street reveals to us a little wine-shop which is said to have been once the home of the "Barber of Seville," whom the novel of Beaumarchais and the opera of Rossini have made immortal. Our carriage can hardly stop anywhere for a moment before it is surrounded by filthy beggars, who form everywhere in Southern Spain an intolerable nuisance. The Spaniards, in their grandiloquent form of speaking, have for these wretches a particular formula, which is supposed to banish them as rapidly as Persian Insect Powder does the pests of Spanish inns. They gravely address these beggars with the words "Perdona usted, por Dios hermano!" "For God's sake, my brother, let your excellency excuse me this time!" Guide-books recommend this phrase, and I tried it several times. It had no other effect than that of turning them from me to the ladies, around whom they crowded like hungry swine. I therefore fell back upon the shorter and much more pointed remark of "Al Demonio!" which usually produced the desired effect, and at the same time relieved my feelings; for it bade them, in plain English, to go to the Devil.

But turning now from the Giralda, let us emerge from the city gates to find ourselves upon the beautiful promenade along the Guadalquivir, whither the fashionable Sevillians invariably resort as day declines. It is a lovely place, indeed. Beside us flows that famous river whose very name, even when pronounced in English, sounds like a strain of music, and on whose ample breast float scores of ships outlining against the evening sky their slender masts, like leafless trees.

Upon the bank, yet close upon the water's edge, you can perhaps discern in the distance an octagonal building called the Tower of Gold. Originally a Moorish structure of defence, it was used by the Spaniards as the treasure-house, where were stored the enormous quantities of gold brought by Columbus and other brave discoverers from the New World. Amid the blare of trumpets and the mad shouts of the exultant populace, the Spanish ships sailed up this

THE GUADALQUIVIR AND THE TOWER OF GOLD.

river, and landed at the base of yonder tower those heaps of shining metal which Spain then fondly deemed exhaustless. Doubtless this brilliant tower was the last object which lingered in the vision of Pizarro, Cortes and Columbus, as they departed from Seville; and likewise formed the brilliant goal of their ambition, as, after years of toil and conquest, they once ascended this river with their precious spoils.

Not far beyond the Tower of Gold let us enter for a moment the grounds of the Duke of Montpensier, whose daughter Mercedes became some years ago the Queen of Spain, and whose untimely death left King Alfonso the most unhappy sovereign of Europe. In some respects this Duke of Montpensier may be called the foremost man in Spain. Ever anxious to introduce improvements, he is found at the head of every useful enterprise. Here, for example, — renewing the system of irrigation which the Moors brought to such perfection, — he has introduced into this park the waters of the Guadalquivir, and thus, as if by enchantment, has made of it a partial vision of the Orient.

GARDEN OF ST. TELMO.

For around us everywhere we now behold the palm — that beautiful symbol of the Orient — the tree of romance and of poetry — the never-to-be-forgotten feature of the East. The first palm-tree ever seen in Spain was planted at Cordova by the noble caliph Abdurrahman the Great, who desired to have here a memorial of his much-loved Damascus. Truly it is not strange that the palm-tree has been worshipped by the children of the sun; for it not only shelters them from the ardent heat, but gives to them unasked the most nutritious fruit, and, surviving through many generations like a beneficent deity, waves over them its rustling boughs as if in constant benediction.

Beneath these palms, however, we woke to the realization that Seville is not always civil. The young Sevillians evidently believe themselves irresistible, or else have a very contemptible opinion of American ladies. In the lovely gardens of San Telmo, on the afternoon of our visit, there chanced to be four or five of these conceited youths, whose cheeks were evidently a battle-field between the contesting forces of whiskers and pimples. It would seem that the charms of the fair ladies accompanying me completely turned the heads of these budding boys. They called aloud to them, "Señoras! Señoritas!" They threw kisses to them from distant terraces. They even extended toward them their arms in theatrical and frantic gestures. In short, they played the rôles of the most ill-mannered simpletons whom it was ever my misfortune to behold.

But now re-entering the city, let us turn to survey one of the most precious monuments of Moorish art in Spain; namely, the Alcazar or Moorish palace, one of whose decorated court-yards we here behold. When the Christians had driven the Moors out of Seville, the conquering monarchs took up their residence here. One of these, Don Pedro the Cruel, wishing to embellish and enlarge this palace, was too wise to employ his own architects for such a work, and accordingly, during a time of peace, sent to Granada for Moorish aid. How beautiful are the results of their labor! Indeed for one who has not seen the Alhambra it is difficult to imagine anything more exquisite than this Alcazar of Seville. For, thanks to the skill and talent of these Moorish workmen, another Aladdin-like palace sprang into existence, almost rivalling the incomparable Alhambra. Here, as there, one fancies himself in some enchanted palace, whose carved and colored walls resemble a continuous network of gold and lace. All is elegance and taste. These arches, not only rest on marble columns; they are beautifully carved and perforated, and even glitter with gilding and vivid colors. The doors too are of cedar-wood inlaid with pearl; around the walls we see a continuous expanse of the Moorish tiles; and all this exquisite work has been recently so carefully restored that it now gleams with almost the same brilliancy and beauty as when it echoed to the footsteps of the Moors.

This charming palace possesses also for every child of the New World an especial interest; for it was here that Queen Isabella gave her private jewels to Columbus, that he might have the means

THE ALCAZAR OF SEVILLE.

requisite for his voyage of discovery. In imagination, therefore, as we stand here, we can almost see the brave-hearted discoverer, his face kindled with the glow of hope regained after years of sad deferment, kneeling before that gracious sovereign, whose wise courage and judicious patronage will ever remain a glorious honor to her memory.

A casket of jewels does not seem much in itself, yet it sufficed in this case to change the destinies of two worlds! But all the souvenirs of this splendid Alcazar are by no means so attractive. Around it cluster also gloomy memories which seem to have no fitness for so fair a spot. These marble pavements have been reddened by the blood of murdered guests, and the dreadful deeds of Don Pedro, whom history has branded with the title of "the Cruel," have rendered forever infamous these decorated halls. It was through this very corridor that, sword in hand, he pursued his brother whom he hated with jealous fury; and here the unhappy victim was at last struck down by the maces of the courtiers; while Don Pedro, coming up to where his brother lay quivering on the pavement, looked at him attentively, and then drawing his dagger handed it to an African slave to give the dying man his death-blow. This done, he calmly re-entered the palace and sat down with invited guests to dinner.

But no description of Seville would be complete without a mention of that thoroughly Spanish sport, — a Bull-Fight. Even in these days of societies for the prevention of cruelty to animals, bull-fighting must still be called the national amusement of the Spaniards, for bull-fights are now patronized by royalty and nobility, and frequented by thousands of men, women and even children, in every large Spanish town.

On one of the first days that I passed in Spain, I found the people in a perfect fever of excitement over the first great bull-fight of the season. Of course it took place on Sunday. All bull-fights do. The theology of the Spaniards is said to be somewhat as follows: As God worked six days and rested on the seventh, so we will rest six days and on the seventh go to the bull-fight. In fact, scarcely has the sunburnt population risen from its knees at mass, when it begins to clamor vociferously, "A los Toros, A los Toros!" "To the Bulls, To the Bulls!" Our guide, Patriccio, was strangely excited. "Come quickly, Señor," he exclaimed, "else I can get you no carriage. All the world goes to bull-fight to-day. Much crowd. Hurry, hurry, dear ladies!"

We scampered down the hotel steps and seated ourselves in a carriage drawn by three gaily decorated mules harnessed abreast. Crack, crack, crack, went the coachman's whip, and away went our mules with their jingling bells, tearing like mad up and down the streets, to the imminent danger of ourselves and everybody else; for all the mules and horses that day were going at full gallop. Soon we were out of the city gate and in the broad avenue leading to the

A SPANISH HERO.

amphitheatre. Tranquil enough it here appears, but on that memorable Sunday afternoon it was swarming with people. The sidewalks were crowded with excited, noisy pedestrians frantic to get ahead. They dared not, however, venture into the street, for that was full of vehicles. And such vehicles! Why, it even surpassed Naples. All sorts of cabs, carts, omnibuses, and showily painted wagons, perfectly loaded down with people, were whirling along (sometimes six abreast) as if their drivers held a direct commission from the Devil.

As we drew near the walls, Patriccio pointed out to me some priests, who are always in attendance here to receive the confession or give the sacrament to any dying bull-fighter. With this cheerful hint of what we were to see, we left our vehicle, which wheeled about while the last one of us was still in the air, and rattled off in quest of other passengers. Then, guided by our skilful Patriccio, we passed within the vast enclosure.

THE ARENA.

The bull ring is built after the style of an old Roman amphitheatre. It is nearly circular in form. Around the arena on the outside are great corridors, with doors opening inwards towards the ring. Our seats were in the second story. We therefore ascended a flight of stairs and passed within the amphitheatre. A striking view outlined itself before us.

Around us on every hand was an unbroken, beautifully curving wall about a hundred feet in height. Below us was the circular arena, and between this and the top of the wall was the most brilliant spectacle imaginable. In the balconies and boxes were gathered no less than *fifteen thousand people !*

Part of these were of course seated in the shade, and part in the sun, as the amphitheatre is entirely open to the sky. The contrast between sunlight and shadow was most beautiful; for where the sunlight fell, six thousand brightly painted fans glittered with all the colors of the rainbow; while in the shade the toilettes of the Spanish ladies, with their lovely black or white lace mantillas, were distinctly visible. It was one of those sights that for an instant make the heart beat almost to suffocation and cause one to catch his breath.

The murmur of thousands of voices, the cries of the venders of oranges and fresh water, and the cheers of eager spectators, as different movements were made preparatory to the combat, all formed a confused roar, comparable to nothing I ever heard before. At length there came a shrill blast of trumpets, the signal for the arena to be cleared of all its lingering occupants. In a few moments the last man had left the enclosure. The arena was empty. Another flourish of trumpets, and in through one of the principal entrances marched the future actors in the bloody drama. At the head came the Picadors, two men on horseback with lance in hand, and dressed in brilliant colors. Next came the Chulos, bearing on their arms the scarlet cloaks with which it would be their duty to enfuriate the bull. These were followed by four or five Banderilléros, who were to act in a way which I shall presently describe. Last of all appeared, in the place of honor, the Matadors, who finally give the bull his death-blow. The costumes of these men are most peculiar. All except the Picadors wear short breeches, silk stockings, and vests and jackets embroidered with silver and gold. Moreover, their hair is very long and is done up in a tight twist behind. After the procession had crossed the arena, it halted in the manner of the old Roman gladiators before the royal box and made a salutation; then it completed the circuit of the ring; the matadors retiring a little from the arena, but the others taking various positions about the wall. Two officers dressed in black and with long nodding plumes in their hats now rode in, and halting before the royal box

3

asked permission of the governor of the spectacle to admit the bull.
The governor threw to them the key of the den where the bull was
confined, and riding rapidly across the arena the officers handed this
to the keeper of the gate. A moment of breathless suspense followed, during which the officers disappeared. Not a sound was
audible. Every eye was fixed on the gateway. Fifteen thousand
hearts were beating with excitement. As for myself, I confess it
was one of the most intensely exciting moments of my life. I cannot
well account for it; but the vast multitude around me, the thought
that I was actually in Spain and about to witness its great national
sport, the dread that I had of its bloody characteristics, and then,
too, the fact that three ladies were with me, who might possibly
faint on my hands — all these combined to agitate me greatly.

At length, almost before I was prepared for it, the gate swung
open and a huge iron-gray bull rushed forth from a perfectly dark
den into the arena. For a moment, astonished and dazzled by the

THE CHULOS.

spectacle around him, and startled by the yells of thousands of
voices, he halted, his nostrils quivering. Then catching sight of
the Chulos, who at a safe distance were waving their red cloaks at
him, he lowered his head and dashed at them with fury. Nimble
as squirrels, these men leaped lightly over the railing of the arena

into a circular space beyond, and the bull stopped with a violent shock within a foot of their retreating heels. With a snort that denoted mischief the bull glared around him. Twenty feet away

THE PICADOR.

was a Picador on horseback. Straight at him the bull now went. The horse, whose eyes were blinded by a cloth, obedient to his rider's spur wheeled to one side, and the Picador pressed his lance into the bull's shoulder as he passed; inflicting only a slight wound, however, for the iron on the lance is purposely made very short. The bull turned savagely about and, irritated by the cut, charged once more upon the horse. Horrible, most horrible! This time the Picador could do nothing, and both horns plunged to the very hilt into the horse's side. Ten thousand voices greeted this with yells of approval. "Bravo, Toro! Bravo, Toro!" resounded in deafening shouts from all parts of the arena. This was bad enough, but I felt almost faint, when I saw the bull actually shake his head up and down, until by his enormous strength he lifted both horse and rider from the ground and rolled them over in the dust. All was now a frenzy of excitement. The bull drew out his dripping horns and prepared for a new charge. If he made it, it would be all over with the Picador. But now the Chulos came to the rescue. Three or four flaunted their cloaks in his face and drew his attention to themselves. As he advanced, however, these agile men slipped aside and the bull struck only the cloaks which passed lightly over his head. While this was being done, other men had assisted the fallen Picador to get upon his feet. He could not have risen without aid; for besides being bruised by his fall, his legs were encased in iron plates of great weight, made to resist the bull's horns.

As for the poor horse, he was left to die in agony, writhing upon the sand, while his life-blood poured out in streams, as he struggled impotently to rise. But by this time the bull had charged in fury upon the other Picador. Almost the same scene was now repeated, save that the bull succeeded in plunging only one horn in the horse's side. Therefore, for the next five or ten minutes, this wretched animal actually galloped about the arena, urged hither and thither by his rider, while his entrails were dragging around his heels and the blood was gushing forth in copious jets! I need hardly say that the ladies of my party shielded their eyes from this horrible sight. A German lady near me wept. But the fair Spaniards seemed to think of nothing but the men and the bull.

The second horse also soon dropped in the agonies of death, and as new Picadors came in, the bull within fifteen minutes had killed three horses outright and horribly wounded a fourth!

He presently stopped as if exhausted. The practised eye of the governor detected now the moment for a change of tactics. He gave a signal, which was followed by a blast from the trumpets. The Picadors at once withdrew from the arena, much to our relief, although the weltering corpses of three horses still lay upon the sand. The Chulos now came prominently forward to take a more decided part in the contest than they had previously assumed, and to perform some of their most daring feats, one of which we here behold, namely, that of jumping over the head of the charging bull, and giving him a love-pat on the neck with the foot in passing!

This they never would have dared to do when the bull was fresh; but now fatigue rendered his charges shorter and more easily avoided. Do you wonder that he was wearied? Up to this time his exertions had been tremendous. The perspiration glistened on his panting sides, while blood coated both shoulders with a crimson mantle, proving that the lances of the Picadors had done their work.

LEAP FOR LIFE.

But a still more daring deed than this was seen, when a Chulo actually ventured to leap over the charging bull by means of a vaulting-pole. Think of the skill and coolness required to leap thus at the right moment! For if he rises too quickly, the bull has an opportunity to halt in time to receive him on his uplifted horns. In any case the pole is almost certain to be knocked from under him, and the man must see to it that he alights upon his feet, or he will be speedily despatched.

But perhaps you ask, "What can induce men to adopt such a foolhardy business as this?" Yet think for a moment of the *fame* they thus acquire. Their names are household words in Spain, and they themselves are looked upon as demigods. Then, too, aside from their magnificent toilettes of silk and satin glittering with gems, their salaries are enormous. The chief Matador, whose duty it is on a Sunday afternoon to kill only two bulls, usually receives for this task about three hundred dollars every Sunday. The men below him also are paid in proportion to the risk they run ; and as these Torreadors are engaged for months ahead in the various amphitheatres, you can easily see that in Spain it is more profitable to kill bulls on Sunday, than in America to preach sermons !

But, after this sport had gone on for some time, a signal was given for a new change of tactics; and the Banderilléros made their

THE BANDERILLÉRO.

appearance to exhibit feats of even greater daring and adroitness. One after another placed himself, as you here observe, before the bull, and goaded him to madness by shaking in his face two colored wands, on the extremities of which were twisted barbs. When the angry animal made a dash at his tormentor, the critical moment came. The Banderilléro waited until the head of the charging beast was within his grasp, and then, *reaching between the advancing horns*, thrust the colored shafts into the shoulders of the bull ! There was a horrible fascination in this spectacle, for it was done just as the bull lowered his head to toss his enemy to the sky. At one moment the man seemed doomed to instant death. The next we saw him leap lightly aside, while the baffled bull fairly bounded up and down under the stab of the two darts, which remained fixed in his bleeding neck. Another Banderilléro now took his position before the bull, and the same exciting scene again took place, until, by a succession of such performances, the wearied and tormented animal bore many of these pointed shafts, which he in vain attempted to shake out of his flesh.

Another flourish of trumpets gave now the signal for the closing scene.

The Matador entered the arena, and, being a special favorite with the public, was received with exultant cheers. With slow and dignified step this admired hero and pet of the ladies advanced to the royal box, and asked permission to kill the bull in a way that should

THE MATADOR.

do honor to all Spain. This being granted, he turned about and faced the bull. In one hand he carried a small red cloak, in the other a strong Toledo sword.

Advancing to within a few feet of the bull, he irritated him a little with the cloak, and pretended to make a few passes, in order to study his wiles. If it be a bold bull which he thus tries, there is little danger, for such an one usually shuts his eyes and madly rushes ahead; but the sly bulls — those which advance and then

retreat, and seek to outwit their antagonists — require close attention. A skilful Matador, however, can always choose the place
where he will lure the bull, and finally kill him; and if the Matador's lady-love be in the amphitheatre, depend upon it, it is always
at the point of the arena nearest her that the bull will die.

At length the bull made a grand rush forward. This was what
the Matador desired. Instead of leaping aside, he planted his feet
firmly, and actually met the monster upon the point of his sword.
But in his thrust consummate skill was shown. It was no ordinary thrust. It is considered a disgrace to stab a bull anywhere
except just at the point of union between the neck and shoulders.
In this case the hand of the Matador was firm and his eye sure, for
the sword was buried to the hilt in the precise spot required; and
while the victor whirled to one side and bowed to the audience, the
bull halted, staggered a few steps, and fell. It was a brave bull,
however, for he refused to die without one more effort. It was
indeed a melancholy sight to see him rise again, drop on his knees,
and give one last brave toss of his great head. Then all that a
moment before was fire, passion and life, fell in an instant — dead —
forever!

Thunders of applause greeted this *dénouement* of the tragedy, and
the gorgeously dressed Matador quitted the amphitheatre, bowing to
the right and left, and evidently feeling himself to be upon the pin-
nacle of glory.

In three minutes the bodies of the dead bull and horses had
been removed from the arena by a train of mules with tinkling bells,
and all was ready for a new combat; for a Sunday afternoon bull-
fight in Spain comprises six distinct tournaments such as I have
described; or if the day be a particularly sacred one, seven bulls are
sacrificed to the populace. The sport is not so monotonous as you
might imagine, for one bull differeth from another bull in glory;
though as a rule they are all fierce and courageous, and kill from
three to six horses each.

We had, however, the somewhat exceptional fortune to see during
the afternoon one cowardly bull. It was the second one to enter the

arena. Instead of charging directly on the Chulos and Picadors, this timid animal ran around the ring seeking some way of escape. Observing this, the Picadors rode directly up to him and pricked him with their lances. Even then the bull would not actually fight, but merely pretended to charge upon the horses, turning away at the last moment without giving the fatal thrust. Then arose a perfect storm of yells, screams and derisive shouts. So great was the noise that it was impossible to make ourselves heard by each other, save by calling as loudly as possible close to the ear.

Oranges were hurled by the score from the audience at the unlucky bull. "Put him out!" "Out with him!" was the verdict of

DEATH IN THE ARENA.

the fifteen thousand spectators. At length this was seen to be a necessity. Chulos and Banderillos could not exasperate him to a charge, and therefore he was ignominiously rejected. A gate opened, and six or eight tame steers were allowed to enter the arena. The coward immediately joined them, when they were all driven out together, and in a moment the ring was ready for the third bull.

But do fatal accidents never occur in these encounters? Not often, strange to say. Yet let us look now on an admirable Spanish work of art, representing a Matador dying in the arena. It reminds me that, as I was observing Frascuelo, — (the greatest of all living Matadors, the pet of Queen Isabella and the present king, — a man who wears diamond shirt studs and a pearl-embroidered jacket in the arena), — Patriccio said to me: " I have often seen Frascuelo in danger, but never so close to death as a few years ago, when, just as he was about to plunge his sword into the bull, the cunning animal, by an unusual toss of his head, jerked the weapon out of the man's hand. Disdaining to run, the Matador stood his ground. On came the bull, and catching the man upon one horn held him there for five minutes, despite all the efforts of the Chulos to free him. At last he flung him into the air. Everybody of course expected to see him fall a mangled corpse. Instead of that, the Matador arose and assured the audience that the bull had not harmed him in the least. The horn had slipped *between his girdle and his shirt !*"

" Did he afterwards kill the bull?" I asked.

" Oh, Señor !" was the reply, " I never saw a bull killed so beautifully ! You see, Frascuelo was so mad, that he thrust his sword in to the very hilt, and held it there till hand and arm were crimsoned."

But from Seville and its bull-fights we now turn impatiently to Granada, the Mecca of our Spanish pilgrimage. In the southern part of the Spanish peninsular lies an enchanting plain some thirty miles in length and bordered by mountains in every direction. Believe me, the whole of Europe has no finer sight than this Granadan plain, green as the richest moss, and ornamented here and there, like Oriental pearls, with white-walled villages and towers. At one end of this unrivalled valley gleams, in the vivid sunlight, the birthplace of ex-Empress Eugenie of France, — the little city of Granada, whose name, some say, is derived from the granates or pomegranates which flourish there now, as they did seven centuries ago, when this was the Moorish Paradise. It is still one of the largest cities of Spain, although its population is but seventy-five thousand as contrasted with four hundred thousand in the time of the Moors. Above the town itself rises abruptly a steep hill not unlike the

Acropolis of Athens, crowned by the old palatial fortress of the Moors, — the favorite home of Moorish Caliphs, their chosen bower of Oriental delights, where life passed away like a happy dream, — the world-renowned ALHAMBRA! The name "Alhambra" appropriately signifies "Red Castle;" for its walls and towers, emerging

THE ALHAMBRA.

from an ocean of green foliage at their base, glow with a beautiful vermilion tint, so different from the blackness with which the hand of Time too frequently enshrouds the ancient edifices of the North.

The ascent to the Alhambra is easy. Broad avenues, often completely embowered in the shade of giant elms, lead the way upward in gradual curves over finely graded terraces. There are certain glorious sensations in the life of every enthusiastic traveller, which in a moment repay him for weeks of absence, privation, and fatigue. No amount of travel can take anything from the thrill of emotion with which one first beholds certain historic sites. Such a spot is the Alhambra, — a gem dimmed and flawed by the rude grasp of many conquerors, but still so incomparably beautiful as to draw to itself admirers from every quarter of the globe. As I rode up this steep ascent and rapidly approached its storied courts, I felt as I did when gliding into Venice, or entering imperial Rome, or when my gaze first rested on the gilded domes of Moscow, or my feet trod the rough pavement of Jerusalem. Nor is the charm here purely one of history; for over these terraces on which we ride stream numerous cascades, in channels framed with ivy leaves and verdant moss. In fact, the music of fountains, or cascades unlocked from the mountain fastnesses above, is sure to greet us here at every turn.

TOWER OF JUSTICE.

Moreover, I found the air as soft and mild as in Greece or Egypt; while the delicious perfume of orange-flowers and roses, which lined the walls at frequent intervals, made breathing a luxury and mere existence a delight. Do not call this rhetoric and exaggeration. I assure you it is only literal truth. Would to Heaven that my words could do justice to this most enchanting of historic spots!

But at length reaching the terminus of these curving driveways, we see before us a large square tower of imposing aspect, the principal entrance to the Granadan Acropolis. It bore the name of the Tower of Justice, because at this gate formerly sat the Moorish sovereign to dispense justice to his subjects, — a custom always common in the East, and one which is mentioned repeatedly in the Hebrew scriptures. An inscription over the doorway reads: "May the Almighty make this portal a protecting bulwark, and write down its erection among the imperishable actions of the just!"

Beneath the arch is an altar consecrated to the Virgin. And it was before this that the first mass was said after the conquest of Granada, while the Moors, with tear-dimmed eyes, were traversing the mountains on their way to Africa.

But hastening through this massive portal, let us enter the Alhambra itself. At once, as though by the magician's spell, we seem

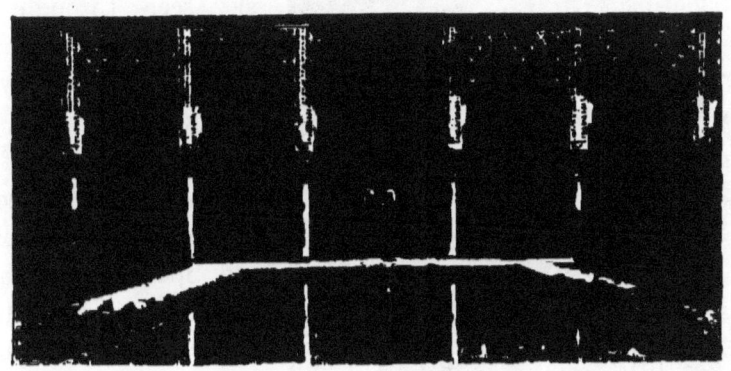

THE COURT OF THE MYRTLES.

to have passed from Europe into Asia! We stand within the Court of the Myrtles. The blue dome of the sky is above us, and beneath are broad marble slabs, whose spotless whiteness was nevertheless once shamed by the snowy feet of the fair Sultanas who lightly trod them; for this was the bathing-place of the wives of the Caliph. In the centre is still the immense marble basin of water, one hundred and thirty feet long and thirty wide, now tenanted by gold-fish and surrounded by hedges of myrtle and orange trees, whose golden fruit glistens among the leaves.

But this is the mere threshold or anteroom of that famous palace whose perfection has rendered it the marvel of the world.

From this, therefore, let us now ascend one or two marble steps to enter the Hall of the Ambassadors. How is it possible for me to describe this room, in which nevertheless I lingered hour after hour during those bright May days? Surrounding us are nine of these windows, piercing the thick Alhambra walls. Their exquisitely chiselled arches seem as unsubstantial as frostwork; while so glorious is the view which they command, that at one of them Charles V. is said to have exclaimed, sighing in pity for the exiled Moor, "Unhappy the man who lost all this!" As for the decoration of these walls, all

HALL OF THE AMBASSADORS.

I could think of, as I beheld them outlined against the azure of the Spanish sky seen through these windows, was a gorgeous mantle of finely woven, cream-colored lace, suspended near a robe of light blue silk. For, indeed, all the designs of the celebrated Spanish lace sold at Granada are copied from the walls of the Alhambra. In the time of the Caliphs this was the grand reception room of the palace. Its floor was of pure alabaster, and an alabaster fountain stood in the centre. It was here also that Washington Irving loved especially to read and write; and I can testify that the swallows, which he described as twittering about the historic hall, still dart in and out through the marble arches, and rest upon the cedar-wood lattices in the high wall, through which doubtless, many a fair Sultana has often gazed, quite unobserved, at the festivities below.

But still better to comprehend the beauty of the walls of the

Alhambra, let us examine a smaller portion of their decoration. We see at once that stucco tapestry expands into intricate designs of gossamer fretwork, which, when colored and gilded in the time of the Moors, must have made of this a veritable Aladdin's palace.

In truth, everything in the Alhambra seems like a fairy tale. Look, for example, at these walls. You fancy them covered with beautiful, but meaningless ornamentation. Not so. Examine them more carefully, and we see not only leaves and flowers budding and blossoming round us in frost-like tracery, but everywhere, interwoven with the vines and flowers, are Arabic inscriptions, meaning: "Blessing," "Welcome," "God is our refuge," "Praise be to God," and, above all, the motto,

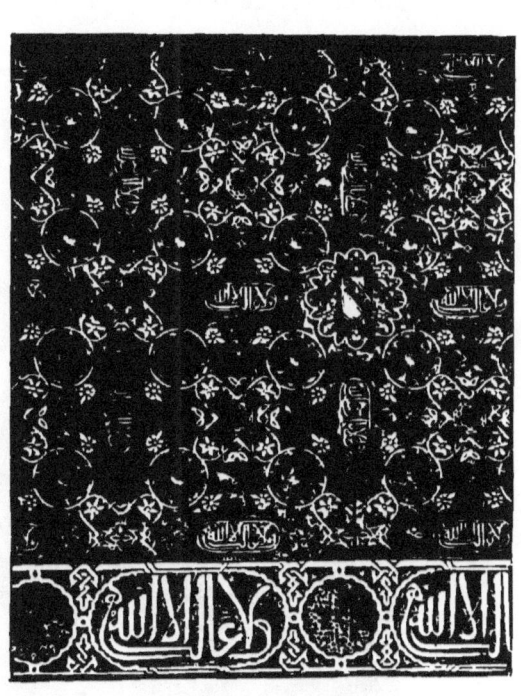

MOORISH DECORATION.

"There is no conqueror but God," — words which the Moorish chieftain answered to his subjects, when they came forth to meet him returning victorious to Granada. In fact, these walls, which were destroyed by the priests as being pagan, are really poems proclaiming the goodness and greatness of God, and forever wedded to the silent music of architecture!

· But if now we turn from the Hall of the Ambassadors, we shall discover, to our infinite regret, that all parts of the Alhambra are not so well preserved as those which we have seen. Through its rude treatment from the hands of man, it has been necessary to support this fragile colonnade with iron bars. These walls also, which here appear so bare and cheerless, were once as exquisitely decorated as those which we have just admired. They have been "*purified*" by the whitewash brush of Isabella's monks! You can still discern, however, cut in the marble steps, a narrow channel, down which in

DESECRATION OF THE ALHAMBRA.

ancient times the water of a fountain ran. For, remember, every room in this palace had its marble fountain; and throughout almost every corridor flowed thus a stream of crystal water, connecting one fountain with another, while filling the air with freshness and the perpetual cadence of a song.

But let us take a step or two to the left and look directly into this apartment, beneath the fretwork of its graceful arches. It is poetically called the "Hall of the Two Sisters," — not, as you might imagine, from any romantic story of two Princesses, but because in the pavement there are two exactly similar marble slabs, of equal purity and beauty. In the distance you can discern two windows at the end of the hall. They look out upon the garden of the Moorish Queen, and as I have sat beside them, enjoying Irving's charming Tales of the Alhambra, I have seen beneath me in that garden the old alabaster fountain, which still pours forth its silver spray, just as it did when its crystal mirror grew lovelier from the reflected features of some fair Sultana.

Standing at one of those windows, one sees to fine advantage the hill which rises opposite to the Alhambra. It is thickly covered with trees and bushes, among which are innumerable caverns cut in the solid rock. These are the homes of the famous Spanish gipsies, who are chiefly found in Andalusia. It would seem that the sun of Southern Spain, which has an almost Oriental splendor, allures these gipsies hither from their native land; for undoubtedly they are of Eastern origin. Until within a few years, they have been unruly members of society, setting at defiance both laws and police; but now they are held to a strict account for their deeds and are also liable to military service. On approaching one of their hillside caverns, a gipsy woman will bring forth to us from a squalid room a cup of coffee, for which we must pay liberally, or else be exposed to great annoyance. The men among these gipsies are for the most part horse-traders and blacksmiths; the women make their fortunes by pretending to tell those of others and by selling fancy articles; while I hardly need add that men, women, and children are all the expertest kind of thieves. In fact, while now we glance at another of these gipsies, whom I met daily in my walks about the Alhambra, let me relate a story which illustrates their cleverness. Some time ago a gipsy, who had been converted to Christianity, was confessing his sins to a priest, when he spied in the monk's pocket a silver snuff-box, and immediately stole it. "Father," he added sorrowfully, "I also accuse myself of having stolen a silver snuff-box."

"Alas! my son," said the good priest, "that is a grievous fault. You must immediately restore it."

"But, Father, will you not take it?"

"I? Certainly not," cried the priest emphatically; "I am not a receiver of stolen goods."

"Well, the fact is," said the gipsy, "I have already offered it to its owner, but he will not take it."

"In that case," said the father, "you can keep it with a clear conscience."

And keep it the gipsy did!

But this is a digression, caused by a view of the gipsy huts from the Alhambra windows. Let us then once more enter the Moorish palace to see its masterpiece and greatest marvel, the famous "Court of the Lions." Here in the very centre of the palace, and surrounded by the rooms which we have thus far seen, is a spacious courtyard, once paved with blocks of snow-white marble, fragments of which remain. Around it on each side are galleries, which are simple marvels of elegance, supported as they are by no less than one

A SPANISH GIPSY.

hundred and twenty-four marble columns, so slender and delicate that they scarcely seem able to bear even the fairy-like arches which rest upon them. These columns were once entirely covered with gold, but after the fall of Granada, instead of repairing them, it was found much more simple and profitable to scrape off all their

THE COURT OF THE LIONS.

gilded ornaments. As some one has well asked, can we not here detect a trace of the former wandering habits of the Moors? In changing their nomadic for a settled life in Spain, did they not imitate in their architecture the luxurious shawls and hangings of their former dwellings, — erecting, instead of a tent pole, a slender

marble column and covering their walls with colors and gilding in
place of the silken tissues of Damascus?

I can truly say that I found the Alhambra to be a marvel, surpassing all my expectations, exalted though they were. Yet if I had
anticipated immense proportions and massive Gothic pillars, I should
have been disappointed. Moorish art has its own distinctive character and conditions, and within them it is unrivalled. Moreover,
we must remember that the Alhambra was a Southern palace, whose
architecture, unlike the Gothic forest of the North, resembles rather
an Oriental flower, glowing with all the vivid colors and redolent with
the sweet perfumes of Asia.

In the centre of this Court of the Lions stands its crowning
beauty, — like a precious stone mounted in a most brilliant setting.
It is an alabaster fountain, the spray from which once fell almost
within the galleries themselves.

The basin of this fountain is one solid piece of alabaster ten
and a half feet in diameter, resting on twelve strangely sculptured
lions, which give its name to the court itself. Around its edge is an
Arabic inscription, on which the eyes of many a Moorish Caliph and
Sultana must have often rested. A portion of it reads as follows:
"Look at this solid mass of pearl spreading through the air its
prismatic shower! One might imagine it to be a block of glistening
ice, with crystal water melting from it." While its concluding
words doubtless express the unuttered prayer of every visitor to the
Alhambra: "The blessing of God be with thee evermore; may thy
pleasures be multiplied, and thine enemies destroyed!"

But perhaps you will exclaim: "How is it possible that the
Moors, whose architecture is unsurpassed for elegance and grace,
could have sculptured such looking animals as these and called them
lions?" It is easily explained. The Koran expressly forbids any
representation of animal life, lest it should lead the Moslems to
idolatry, — thus cutting them off at once from both painting and
sculpture, in which perhaps the Arabs would have excelled as wonderfully as in architecture. I think, however, that these beasts could
be safely worshipped, without at least violating one of the old Hebrew

Commandments; for they resemble nothing either in heaven above, or the earth beneath, or in the waters under the earth.

It was in the shade of these marble galleries that the Moorish monarch and his friends loved to pass the midday hours, enjoying the murmur of fountains and the cool air of the Alhambra heights. And we are told that the Moorish ladies, whose beauty lent to this incomparable edifice an added charm, were finely formed, graceful in their manners, and fascinating in their conversation. The Arab poets say of them, indeed, that when they smiled they displayed teeth of dazzling whiteness, while their breath was like the perfume of flowers.

LIFE IN THE ALHAMBRA.

It was standing in this Court of the Lions that my guide Mariano said to me, as we paused to listen to the song of a nightingale in the foliage beyond, "In those notes we fancy that we hear the voices of the lost Sultanas, whose spirits still return to haunt their earthly Paradise!" Each part of the Alhambra is haunted thus by some poetic legend, many of which have been inimitably told by Irving.

One of its towers, for instance, filled even now with exquisite Moorish tracery, is called the "Tower of the Captive;" because within its walls was once imprisoned a fair Christian captive, whom the Moorish sovereign wished to add to his Harem. Finally in despair she flung herself from its lofty window, beneath which her lifeless form was found by her lover, who came at last — too late to rescue her.

It was by moonlight in this lovely court that I took my farewell look at this gem of Moorish art and Oriental beauty.   The rays of

THE "LAST SIGH OF THE MOOR."

the crescent moon (the glorious symbol of Islam), striking these slender pillars obliquely, gave to them the transparency of alabaster, yet clothed them with a dust of gold.   Through the perforated carvings of the galleries the moonbeams darted in like silver arrows, as if to pierce the once richly gilded capitals of the marble shafts.

As I gazed, I felt as though I were removed from the world of reality, and were wandering in a moonlit palace of alabaster in the time of the Arabian Nights.

But now, emerging from the palace itself, let us climb to the top of one of the Alhambra towers, and look far off upon the undulating wall of mountains which surrounds it. Most of these peaks are tawny and picturesque in their desolate grandeur, while one of them is peculiarly interesting from its name and history. It is called the "Last Sigh of the Moor," because when Boabdil, the last of the Moorish kings, was fleeing from his beloved city, he paused upon that summit to take a farewell look at the Alhambra and its incomparable plain. The last Moorish gem had then been transferred to the Spanish crown. The Christian banner floated on his rose-hued towers, and all was lost. What wonder that he wept in anguish, exclaiming, "God is great, but when did ever misfortune equal mine?" And, in fact, behind him lay the most exquisite situation upon earth. Before him lay the desert of Africa, as cheerless as the prospects of a dethroned fugitive. Yet his mother imbittered his grief by exclaiming, "You weep now like a woman over what you could not defend as a man!"

But the crowning glory of this wondrous view from the Alhambra is the chain of the Sierra Nevada, covered with dazzling snow, and piercing the blue sky at a height of eleven thousand feet! Rightly did the Arab poets compare these mountains to a sparkling mass of mother-of-pearl,—a vision never to be forgotten. They have been the pride of Granada ever since from their sparkling heights fleet horsemen used to bring ice in baskets to cool the wine of the Moorish kings. Beautiful in form and color, they stand above this Damascus of the West like beneficent deities, fanning her with cooling breezes, tempering her summer heat, and feeding her limpid rivers from an unfailing treasure-house of snow. And now, by contrast, let us transport ourselves in imagination from this former to the present home of the Moors, and stand in one of their stately olive-groves near Morocco. Alas! the glory of the Moors is now departed. Little remains to them save bitter memories. Surely it is not strange that with such a glorious past behind them, — connected too with the fairest spot on earth, — the grief of the exiled Arabs is still pathetically sad. With the exception of the Jews, there is not another such case as theirs in history. Spain still appears to them as a

"HE THINKS OF GRANADA."

"Paradise Lost." It is said that one very distinguished Arab family, not many miles from Tunis, still keeps the key of the old ancestral mansion in Granada. And to this day, among the degenerate Moors of Africa, when one of their number is pensive or sad, his comrades will whisper, as they point to him, " *He thinks of Granada !*"

Filled with such memories, let us now return to Spain, and follow rapidly in the footsteps of the retreating Moors until we reach the shores of the Mediterranean. Before us rises, sombre and threatening, to the height of seventeen hundred feet, the Rock of Gibraltar, crouched like a monstrous sphinx upon the border of the sea, and guarding thus the most important gateway of the world. Although completely paved with English cannon and surmounted by the British flag, this mountain is still an eloquent memorial of the Arabs ; for Gibraltar is only a corruption of Gibel-al-Tarif, — the mountain of Tarif, the leader of the Moors when they first landed in Spain. Still more impressive does this cliff become when we behold it flushed with the radiance of the sunset glow. What wonder that the ancients called this the gilded pillar of Hercules, planted by the gods at the western extremity of the universe, beyond which even the boldest never dared to sail ?

As we look upon this golden gateway of the West, while the waves of two oceans break in ceaseless cadence at its feet, we remember with a sudden pang of regret that for us the fascinating book of

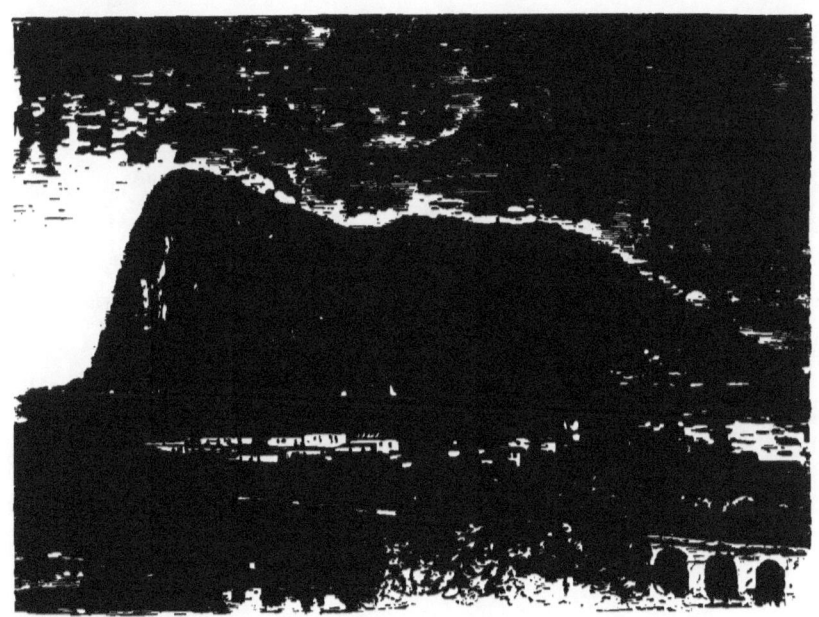

THE ROCK OF GIBRALTAR.

Spanish travel is closing fast. Farewell, vermilion towers of Granada; farewell, embroidered walls of the Alhambra; sweet orange-groves of Andalusia; fair Giralda of Seville; and marble forest of the Mosque of Cordova! It is a joy forever to have seen you. For hereafter in the picture galleries of our memories there will hang no more brilliant and alluring tableaux than those which are tinted by the sun of Spain.

THE PASSION PLAY
OF OBER-AMMERGAU ✝
✸ 1880

THE PASSION PLAY AT OBER–AMMERGAU IN 1880.

I SOLATED from the rest of the world by a lofty barrier of mountain ranges, and hidden far away in one of the picturesque valleys of the Tyrol, lies that little Bavarian village now known throughout the world under the name of Ober-Ammergau.

Thither, through motives of curiosity or piety, about two hundred thousand men and women, during the summer of 1880, made their way.

The cause of this marvellous influx of travellers was no magnificent cathedral, no picturesque ruin, nor even mediæval castle; for none of these does the little town possess. The sole attraction there was the performance of its world-renowned Passion Play. And what is this marvellous Passion Play, which has thus been able to draw to itself, through difficulties and hardships, thousands of people whom no other dramatic scene could possibly have enticed a hundred miles from their own firesides? It is a relic of mediæval Christianity,—a legitimate descendant of the so-called Miracle Plays common throughout Europe six or seven hundred years ago. Now, the world in general has outgrown these plays. They were doubtless useful in their time, as vivid object lessons, but, with the birth and growth of printing, the period of their utility gradually passed away. Yet, much as the ancient religions of Greece and Rome survived for generations in the villages, long after they had been superseded in the cities by another creed (thus stamping the ancient faith with the name *Pagan*, from *paganus*, a rustic), so in this remote valley of Bavaria we still see the Passion Play surviving all its

kindred, like the last sacred fire kindled on a neglected shrine by
the ardent breath of simple piety.   In all probability some drama
of Christ's life was performed at various times in this secluded vale
as early as the thirteenth century, but it became an established
institution there only two hundred and fifty years ago.   Then, tradition tells us, the ancestors of the present villagers made a solemn
vow that if God would check a plague at that time raging in their
midst, they would thereafter perform every ten years the drama
of Christ's life and sufferings.

The plague having abated, these people have therefore ever since
considered themselves sacredly bound to carry out this vow of their
forefathers, bequeathing it from generation to generation as a precious
and sacred legacy.   It is true, the form of the play has of late years
been carefully revised and shorn of many crudities by the intelligent
pastor of the village, Daisenberger; but the substance of it still remains
intact, and now, therefore, Ober-Ammergau is the only place where any
remnant of the real mediæval Passion Play is still performed with all
the simplicity and reverence of ancient days.

I hardly need add that the so-called "Passion Play," which, in
obedience to public sentiment, has been recently withdrawn from the
New York stage, has nothing whatever to do with this Play at Ober-
Ammergau.   That was a purely modern drama written by Mr. Salmi
Morse, and possessing neither the music nor the text of the Bavarian play, nor even the arrangement of its parts, while it was of
course wholly lacking in its remarkable religious traditions and
historical associations.

The approach to Ober-Ammergau on the days immediately preceding a performance is not such as to put one in a very devotional
frame of mind.   I shall not soon forget the excited crowd gathered
at the railway station in Munich on a certain Friday morning in
July; nor the grand stampede which occurred when the train was
finally ready to receive us; nor the frantic struggling for seats on
the part of hundreds of pilgrims; nor the long array of more than
thirty cars, in which, packed like diminutive fishes whose name I

need not mention, we crept along during four terribly tedious hours. All this can be easily imagined. But what never will and never can be adequately conceived, is the confusion attendant on the disembarkation of all these travellers at the railway terminus. In fact, picture to yourselves the wild hubbub occasioned by seven or eight hundred people alighting at a country village all at once in a pouring rain, and searching for carriages to convey them sixteen miles further to Ober-Ammergau! Not that there were not vehicles

GOING TO OBER-AMMERGAU.

enough! Oh, no! the supply, such as it was, proved equal to the demand; for every town in the vicinity had sent thither not only all its good carriages, but also every old chaise, wagon, tip-cart, and hayrack whose parts could still hold together. These were drawn out before the station in a gigantic line, presenting an appearance which defies description. As I looked at them, I felt as if I had come to attend the funeral of the whole German nation, or else was about to participate in a colossal procession of " Antiques and Horribles." But let us now suppose that our three hours' ride in one of these conveyances is approaching its conclusion, and that from a distance we are looking on the little village itself, nestling at the very base of lofty mountains thousands of feet in height. Especially prominent among these is the central peak of the Kofel, directly overhanging the village church, and crowned, as you can perhaps discern, by

THE VALLEY AND THE KOFEL.

a gigantic cross cutting its simple outline sharply on the sky. This mighty cross seems indeed the presiding genius of the place; for it is bright with the kiss of dawn an hour before the mists of morning quit the valley; and long after evening has enfolded the village in its dusky mantle, with outstretched arms resplendent in the sunset glow it seems bestowing on the peaceful vale its benediction.

But ere we fairly enter this pretty hamlet, we pause to examine a colossal group of statuary placed on the hillside just outside the town. It was presented five years ago to the people of Ober-Ammergau by the King of Bavaria as a mark of his appreciation of their piety. It attracts our attention, however, not so much as the gift of a king, or even as a work of art, — though it is not undeserving of praise, — but on account of a pathetic incident connected with it.

KING LUDWIG'S GIFT.

A few years since, as this group was being drawn up the extraordinarily steep mountain road leading to Ober-Ammergau, the wagon containing it slipped back a little, and this figure of St. John was thrown out. Unhappily, it fell upon the sculptor and his assistant, crushing the former to death upon the spot, while his assistant died the next day in great agony. There was therefore something peculiarly horrible to me in the sight of this nobly designed statue of St. John; for, notwithstanding its beauty, I could but feel, in beholding it, as though the insensate stone were a moral agent and had committed parricide in taking thus the life of the author of its being.

But, riding now beyond this group, let us approach the village still more closely. Impatient as we are to enter it, let me detain you a moment longer at the threshold beneath the towering summit of the Kofel, while I answer a question existing probably in the mind of every visitor to Ober-Ammergau; namely, How will it be possible for common peasants to interpret with any skill and power, or even to appreciate, so lofty a theme as the Passion Play? But in reply, let me say at once that the chief actors here are by no means "common peasants." Joseph Maier, for example, who takes the part of the Christ, and the impersonators of Judas, Pilate, and other leading characters, are in reality artists, who support themselves and their families by wood-carving, many of their productions being very beautiful and praiseworthy.

In fact, there is in this secluded mountain region a permanent school of design and carving, aided by the Bavarian Government, and supported by the inhabitants often at a severe pecuniary sacrifice. All this gives them an æsthetic education in itself; and its influence upon the villagers is seen in their taste for decoration, and the natural correctness of grouping and the artistic postures which they assume upon the stage.

This drama of the passion of Christ not only forms in its long preparation and enactment a considerable part of the individual lives of these villagers, but is also the central feature in the history of the village itself. For their various parts in it they are often trained by gradual steps from childhood to old age, and, profiting by centuries of stage traditions, they come to the rendition of their characters with a wonderful enthusiasm and religious fervor. Not to be considered fit to appear at all in the Passion Play would be for an Ober-Ammergau peasant a terrible misfortune and disgrace; while to enact the part of the Christ is the noblest honor of which he can conceive. Moreover, we must not make the mistake of supposing Ober-Ammergau to be an ordinary German village. In some respects it is entirely unique and remarkable. Not only is this Passion Play performed here at the recurrence of each decade, but every year upon a permanent stage these villagers enact at frequent intervals, for their own education, recreation, and improvement, not merely religious dramas, but also such noble plays as those of Schiller and Goethe, and even the Greek Antigone of Sophocles, adapted for them by their venerable pastor. Thus they acquire continual dramatic training, and are raised to a high standard of appreciation.

This being premised, let us without further delay pass within the town itself. I was quite pleasantly disappointed in its appearance, the white stone houses being unusually neat and clean. The religious character of the place is shown at once by the fact that many of the houses have highly colored frescos on their outer walls, representing Biblical or sacred mediæval legends. On some of the buildings, however, I discerned a much more prosaic view of life in the

VILLAGE OF OBER-AMMERGAU.

notice that there coffee and lager beer could be obtained. But what astonished me chiefly on entering the town was my sudden advent into saintly society. Hardly had our carriage passed within the first street, when the driver pointed out to us the residence of Judas. A few paces further on, stood a man in his shirt-sleeves, pumping water. "That," whispered my coachman, "is St. John." Before I could fairly look at him, my attention was called to Herod, whose occupation is that of a baker, and whose bare arms were white with

flour.   I was trying to remember that of course these simple peasants could not always go about the streets in their stage costumes,
when a boy, whose long hair was streaming out in all directions, as
though he had taken a shock of electricity, came running out of
a neighboring doorway.   This proved to be the youthful Joseph,
who was forced by his elder brethren to carry my valise for me,
and even to black my boots while I lodged in his father's house.
But through these village streets we naturally make our way as
soon as possible to the theatre itself.   Certainly one could imagine
nothing plainer.   It looked to me very much like the exterior of

EXTERIOR OF THEATRE.

a cattle-fair or race-course, especially when thousands of peasants
were assembled here struggling to gain admission.   In fact, up to
the time of my passing inside the walls, I confess to having expe-
rienced here little else than feelings of disappointment and disgust ;
for, notwithstanding the most extraordinary precautions on my part,
and a wonderful amount of kindness exercised by friends already in
the village, we had found on our arrival our positively engaged
apartments already given up to others.   And may Heaven preserve
my worst enemy from such a fate as that in an over-crowded German hamlet !   We had, therefore, passed our first night at Ober-
Ammergau in vile quarters, characterized by an odor which I should

suppose must also have pertained to Noah's ark after the forty days' rain, when only one window could be opened for ventilation. Moreover, that same night had been rendered sleepless by desperate conflicts with those tiny animals which form, alas, the curse of Southern Europe. Even the second night, also, though spent in clean apartments, had been as noisy as, in this country, the night preceding the Fourth of July. For, from the early hour of three o'clock Sunday morning, our slumbers had been broken by the sounds of bells, horns, guns, innumerable voices, and finally a band of music. Then, too, so crowded was the town that, on looking out of my window at daybreak, the first thing I discovered was a gentleman completing his toilet in a carriage where he had passed the night! When, therefore, at half past seven Sunday morning, I stood before this uninviting theatre, my spirits were not buoyant; and if any one had then told me that I should describe the Passion Play itself as I shall

now proceed to do, I should have laughed him to scorn. But, forgetting these minor tribulations, before we take our seats within the auditorium, let us in imagination pass behind the scenes, and observe some of the principal actors ere they make their appearance on the stage. And, first, while looking on the face of the spirited performer who took the part of Joseph of Arimathea, let me answer a question continually addressed to me in reference to the pecuniary results of the Passion Play. "What is done with

JOSEPH OF ARIMATHEA.

the money?" it is asked, and "Who receives it?"

This Herr Maier explained to me quite fully. The money received from the sale of tickets, varying as they do in price from twenty-five cents to two dollars, is divided into four parts. The first is used to pay off the expenses of the season, one item of which (that of the costumes) cost in 1880 fourteen thousand dollars. The second quarter is laid aside as a permanent fund, to improve the town and to build a new theatre at the expiration of the next ten years. The third part is devoted to the church and to the poor of the village. The last is divided among some seven hundred actors!

HEROD.

The statement has been made that Joseph Maier was greatly dissatisfied with his pecuniary receipts for the season of 1880. I believe this to be erroneous, because at that time he said repeatedly that he should be perfectly content if he received for his whole summer's work (and remember that he has acted his part every Sunday and Monday from May to the last of September) *one hundred dollars!* Ten years ago he received even less than this. It is difficult to obtain a reliable estimate of the amounts paid to him and to the other performers; but, as rumor places Maier's receipts for the season at more than two hundred dollars, I believe him to be more than satisfied, in accordance with his own declaration.

But now, for a moment, let us observe another of these actors, who assumes the part of Herod. The sight of this man reminds me that I may here appropriately answer another question frequently asked in regard to these villagers; namely, Have they not been made worldly, possibly even corrupt, by the multitude of strangers flocking to their secluded town? If any man in Ober-Ammergau could have made me think so, it is this same impersonator of King Herod; for it was in his house that I at first lodged, and, as I have already hinted, both he and his wife seemed best fitted to play the rôles of

Ananias and Sapphira, having flagrantly (and I think inexcusably) broken their word in regard to my promised rooms. Moreover, in the controversy which ensued between us, this man became so extremely violent and abusive, not only to myself but to a lady of my party, that I suspected him of being capable of another murder of the innocents, and appealed to the Burgomeister of the village for assistance. This he most willingly gave, deciding immediately in my favor. Now, if I were to judge all the villagers by this one instance, I should certainly give them a bad reputation.

But on account of this very difficulty I took unusual pains to study the people of Ober-Ammergau without prejudice, and am convinced that Herod was an exception to the rule. His violent character seemed to be well known in the town, and his neighbors spoke of him as possessed of an unfortunate and ungovernable temper. Moreover, it is only justice to say that this disagreeable experience was abundantly offset by the unselfish kindness of another of the actors, who apologized with tears in his eyes for the discourtesy which had been shown to us by one of his townsmen, and insisted

PETER.

upon giving up to us his own room during our stay in Ober-Ammergau, though at great inconvenience (as I afterwards learned) to himself and a relative whom he had invited to lodge with him.

Yet, while we glance at Jacob Hett, the dignified actor who, both in 1870 and 1880, has assumed the rôle of Peter, let me add that undoubtedly human nature is much the same the world over, and every country town (especially when exposed to a weekly avalanche of twelve thousand visitors) will inevitably present some disagreeable characteristics. The people of

Ober-Ammergau are not entirely unlike other people, and therefore they of course expect to earn some money from the entertainment of their guests. This is but natural and proper. No one, certainly, should grudge them the little they thus gain, once in ten years, by hard labor and great discomfort to themselves and families. But that these people give the Passion Play itself from mercenary motives, is an idea which no unprejudiced observer will, I think, for a moment entertain. It is a well-known fact that they have refused several very tempting offers to perform in England and America.

The sum of thirty thousand dollars was offered these villagers, if a few of their number would act the Passion Play in Vienna during the exposition of 1873. This also they refused. Herr Maier himself expressed in my presence the greatest indignation at the idea that their sacred and historic drama should thus be made an article

MARY.

of speculation in the markets of the world, adding that if the Passion Play were not performed in 1890, it would be on account of the corrupt and worldly influence of outside adventurers and speculators.

But now, before the drama actually commences, let us look at the face of her who during the summer of 1880 assumed the part of Mary, the mother of Jesus.

It certainly is not the conventional Madonna's face. We cannot even call it beautiful. Yet her features are marked by tenderness and refinement, though care and toil have evidently left deep traces there. The female characters of the Ober-Ammergau Passion Play, as last enacted, formed, however, the weakest feature of the drama. The women did not compare with the men in dramatic ability, and labored under the great disadvantage of having to strain their voices to make themselves heard across the vast auditorium. Nevertheless, in the part of Mary there was happily little to criticise. Her anxiety, her love, and agony of mind were all portrayed, with considerable power, and with much delicacy of interpretation. There was, at all events, no ranting or extravagance in her acting, which, considering the tendency to excess that we might naturally expect here, was all the more remarkable.

But, having thus satisfied ourselves with a glimpse at those actors whose parts we shall not prominently trace throughout the play, let us hasten, with thousands of others, within the theatre itself.

At once its barn-like exterior gives place to an immense auditorium and stage, usually severely plain, but in some places tastefully

INTERIOR OF THEATRE.

decorated. The stage is entirely uncovered, and thus the actors are exposed alike to sun and rain. The greater part of the auditorium also is open to the sky, only some hundreds of cane-seated chairs in the rear

THE CHORUS.

being protected by a canopy. The passage-ways upon the right and left of the stage represent streets in Jerusalem; while between them and the drop-curtain in the centre the two houses with balconies typify, respectively, the dwellings of Pilate and Annas, the High Priest. The impression produced from the very outset was remarkable; for at least six thousand people were gathered here in eager expectation of what they were to see; and on one side, as we awaited the opening of the drama, we could look forth upon lofty mountains, and on the other, over and beyond the stage, upon a charming expanse of the Ammergau valley; the beauty of the landscape, the vistas of mountains and valleys, waving trees, blue sky, and fleecy clouds imparting a delightful air of freshness and enchantment to the scene.

It was precisely eight o'clock when a cannon woke with its reverberations the echoes of the neighboring mountains, and gave the signal for the drama to commence. As in an ordinary theatre, the director of the orchestra raised his baton, and the first strains of a solemn overture floated out upon the silent air. This was the visible prelude to the play; but there was also a prelude which was by us unseen; for during the performance of the overture, behind the curtain of the central stage, all the principal actors were assembled together with their pastor, engaged in silent prayer. At length, the preliminary music being concluded, a company of nineteen persons made their appearance, arrayed in brightly colored robes and mantles. With slow, dignified step they advanced, to stand in a slightly concave line across the entire stage. They represent a company of guardian spirits, who throughout the entire play perform almost precisely the duty of the old Greek chorus in the Athenian dramas; that is to say, their duty is to announce and explain the various scenes and tableaux, as well as to impress upon the audience their moral lesson; for, as their name implies, they must be continually present, as heavenly monitors, during the entire performance.

Now, there are in the Passion Play eighteen acts, before and after

TABLEAU.

each of which this chorus sings; and, since in the mind of the Ober-Ammergau villagers the explanation of these spiritual guardians is not sufficient, at the conclusion of their chant the singers gracefully retreat to right and left, and the curtain rises in the centre to disclose a tableau, supposed to be typical of the scene which is to follow. Thus tableaux, dramatic scenes, and sacred chants glide one into another all day long, without the slightest hesitation. For example, the tableau now before us represents Adam toiling for his bread in the sweat of his brow, and precedes the act where Christ endures the anguish of Gethsemane. Another, which portrays Joseph sold into captivity by his brethren, precedes and typifies the act wherein we see the betrayal of Jesus by Iscariot. In the same manner, the remorse of Judas for his treachery has a tableau pre-

ceding it, where Cain is portrayed as rushing forth from the murder
of his brother, the curse of the Almighty on his brow. Many of
these tableaux are most remarkable, not only from the great multitude of participants, (numbering, as they sometimes do, *four or five
hundred persons*), but also from the really wonderful statue-like
repose observed by all of them, even to the little children of two
or three years of age. In one of these tableaux were at least one
hundred and fifty children; yet, through a powerful glass I was
unable to detect in them the slightest movement, even when fully
five minutes had elapsed between the rising and falling of the
curtain !

ENTRY INTO JERUSALEM.

But now we are naturally impatient for the first act of the drama
itself. Scarcely has the chorus left the stage after its first appearance, when the air is filled with shouts of rejoicing, and down the
streets of Jerusalem we see a vast multitude of men, women, and
children eagerly advancing, waving palm branches, and shouting
"Hosanna !" as the Christ makes his triumphal entry into the city,
riding upon an ass.

Only a small portion of this multitude is represented in the illustration, for if the whole stage were portrayed, the figures would be microscopic; but it serves to give us a suggestion of what the entire scene must be. If it be thrilling to witness, on an ordinary stage, as in the play of Julius Cæsar, a moving multitude of fifty or sixty actors, think of the effect produced by *five or six hundred* men, women, and children, all clad in bright Oriental costumes, singing and shouting together in exultation, all moving in the vivid sunlight and under the open sky, so that one fancies he is witnessing an actual procession in the streets! In the midst of this vast concourse we discern the figure of the Christ (Joseph Maier), surrounded by some of his disciples. At this point began my first feelings of amazement at the Passion Play. I had expected very ordinary acting, if not in the leaders, at least in those who sustained the minor parts. But, without the slightest qualification, I can truly say that in none of the great theatres of the world have I seen in an operatic chorus or crowd of theatrical performers anything like the *freedom and naturalness* of these multitudes of Ober-Ammergau. I attribute this chiefly to two causes, — first, the incessant practice which they have undergone for days and months and years; and second, the fact that such large numbers naturally inspire confidence in the individual actors, preventing even the most timid from appearing embarrassed or constrained.

As for the Christ himself, who has made his triumphal entry into the Holy City, let us examine his face separately. Throughout the drama we shall behold many representations of Maier with very different expressions, but they are all full of interest.

The one before us indicates his attitude, when, after alighting from the ass, he enters the temple and looks upon the desecration of his Father's house. His face expresses indignation, but indignation mingled with profound grief. In the whole course of the drama I think there is nothing which puts the delicate appreciation of Maier more to the test than this scene in the temple with the money-changers. Think of the opportunity here afforded for ranting and extravagance, especially when he overturns the tables of the traders and those who sell doves, and drives them forth with a whip of cords!

A single bad gesture, a single violent or vulgar movement, would be here revolting. But Maier is equal to the test.

CHRIST IN THE TEMPLE.

Advancing slowly and with a certain majestic sadness, which I cannot sufficiently praise, he pushes aside the tables, not in hasty anger, but rather as though their presence were pollution ; and we are so absorbed by his look and action that we hardly notice when they really fall. Perhaps we should not do so, were it not that real doves thus loosened from their cots fly over the walls of the auditorium into the adjoining town.

This, indeed, is an illustration of the fact that throughout his entire rôle Maier looks upon the character of Jesus from a divine, rather than a human, standpoint. Even in his most thrilling moments he is always self-controlled. Never for an instant does he lose the sublime consciousness of his high mission; and even with his humility there is mingled a certain grandeur. But a still more difficult task is that which Maier encounters in the scene of the Last Supper. Here also I could discover, in his bearing, his action, and the perfect enunciation of his words, absolutely nothing to criticise.

The grouping here of Maier and his disciples, as you at once discern, closely resembles Leonardo da Vinci's well-known painting of this subject. In fact, it reproduces that picture in life, with all its richness of Oriental coloring.

The scene is one of great beauty and impressiveness, especially when, the dispute having arisen among the disciples as to which shall be chief, the master rises with inimitable dignity and reproachful love, and slowly passes from one to another, to set them the

example of humility by washing their feet.   You can better realize
the intensity which Maier throws into his acting here, when I tell
you that he said to a friend of mine, "You cannot imagine how I
come to love those men at the Last Supper, while I am washing
their feet."   This action seems to touch profoundly even the heart
of Judas; for he sits for some time after with his head resting on
his hands, as though still struggling with his conscience.

During the distribution of the bread and wine the silence of the
immense audience seems breathless; the climax being reached when

THE LAST SUPPER.

the announcement is made by Jesus, "Verily, verily, I say unto you,
that one of you shall betray me!"

In the consternation which follows, even Judas himself, confused and fearful, exclaims with the others, "Lord, is it I?"   And
Maier answers him sadly, yet not without some sternness in his
voice, "Judas, that which thou doest, do quickly."   While speaking thus of Iscariot, let us now look upon his face.   Next to
Maier he is undoubtedly the finest of the actors.   His features mark
him as a man of strong character, and at no time in the drama
does he fail to command our interest and sympathy.   For, from
the first moment, when the hideous idea of betraying his master
for money is suggested to him by the agents of the chief priests,

until his remorse culminates in suicide, his rendering of his part is wonderful.

Now, Gregor Lechner, who in 1870 as well as 1880 has taken this rôle, is a most worthy man, and hence he feels it keenly that

JUDAS.

so many (especially of course among the peasants) identify his assumed, with his real, character. Many people, indeed, actually refuse to buy his portrait with those of the other actors, and look upon him with unconcealed abhorrence.

By a singular coincidence, Lechner's father also took the part of Judas forty years ago. When, therefore, the present actor was recently asked if he was training his bright little son, who is in the tableaux, to follow him in the rôle of the betrayer, he emphatically replied, "No! I have suffered already too much in the eyes of the people to wish my child to assume the part."

But now let us look upon some prominent features in the rôle of Judas: and first, the scene with the Sanhedrim. The rising curtain reveals the assembled council. Judas has not yet made his appearance before them. Caiaphas and Annas occupy the central seats of honor, above the tables of the scribes. A most exciting debate is being carried on, as to what shall be done with this Galilean, the words uttered being such as must naturally have been spoken on the occasion. In fact, I may here remark parenthetically that whenever the text of the Passion Play leaves the direct narration of the Gospels, the language is usually simple, dignified, and often eloquent.

The High Priest, Caiaphas, (who in private life is Burgomeister of the village), is richly attired in a long white robe with silver fringe, while on his breast gleam the twelve jewels symbolic of the Israelitish tribes.

It is he who first addresses the assembly with passionate eagerness. "Fathers of the people," he exclaims, "our religion is in danger of being overthrown. Did not this Galilean drive out the buyers and sellers from the temple? Did you not see how he entered our city in triumph? He is carrying the people with him and is teaching them to despise us. Shall we wait here until the last shadow of our power is gone? I, at least, am in favor of his death." The aged Annas also rises from his seat and exclaims, in tones tremulous

ISCARIOT AND THE SANHEDRIM.

with emotion and infirmity, "By my gray hairs, I swear not to rest, until our religion is made safe by his destruction."

At length, they fully decide to put the Nazarene to death; but of this, when Judas makes his appearance, they cunningly say nothing. On the contrary, they tell him only that they wish to imprison his master for a short time, to prevent his uttering any more extreme doctrines.   Judas stands for some moments thus, beside a little table in the centre, listening to the words of the council, and struggling with his feelings.   His acting here is exceptionally fine.

Without uttering a single word, he yet makes it perfectly evident that what he is about to do is revolting to his better nature.   The sight of the money, however, and its ring upon the table decide him; and, as if lured on by an irresistible attraction, he clutches the silver, tests each piece, and sweeps it eagerly into the bag.   Meantime his evil genius (the agent of the chief priests) stands watching him intently, as Mephistopheles watches Faust, lest at the last moment he may recoil.

Another very striking feature in the part of Judas is his conduct in the betrayal scene, which we will now pass to consider.   The rising curtain reveals the Garden of Gethsemane, whither Maier has led the disciples from the Last Supper.   There was to me nothing more touching in the whole drama than Maier's acting in this scene.   One naturally trembles at first with apprehension, lest he do something which shall offend; but all such anxiety is needless while Joseph Maier takes the part of Christ.   Three times he goes away to kneel in prayer; three times, in a tone which thrills us with sympathy, he pleads, " Father, if it be possible, let this cup pass from me;" but finally, when he has gained the spiritual victory, there falls from his lips the sublime expression, " Father, not as I will, but as thou wilt!"

Then for a moment there appears an angel strengthening him. Meantime his disciples are sleeping on, unmindful of their master's agony.   He looks upon them sadly yet tenderly, as one might look upon a weary child.   Then, as though foreseeing the trials which await them, he murmurs, " Sleep on now and take your rest;" but soon arouses them with the words, " Arise! for the hour is at hand!" It is indeed time.   The Roman guards have come, and, guided by the faithless Judas, have surprised the Christ and his disciples in the shadows of Gethsemane.   Iscariot advances with a rapid step, like one who is forcing himself in desperation to some hateful act which he has promised to perform.   Here again his manner perfectly portrays the partial loathing with which he regards his treachery.   With a quick, convulsive movement he seizes the hand of his master, and imprints upon his pallid cheek the fatal kiss. Then, with an appearance of relief and partial shame, he skulks away among the trees and lets the Roman soldiers do their work. There is something sublime in the isolation of Maier, as he stands thus looking on the soldiers who

THE BETRAYAL.

recoil before his glance. All the weakness and irresolution of the previous hour have vanished. Calm and collected, he confronts them like a captive king. But his disciples, who an hour before had been so loud in their protestations of devotion even unto death, all hurry off in terror through the shadows of the garden, leaving him alone.

But let us look upon Judas in one last illustration of his part.
We see him here experiencing the tortures of a guilty conscience,
and his remorse, expressed in words, in gesture, and in act, is simply
terrible.   When he learns that Jesus is condemned to death; when
he rushes into the presence of the priests and begs in piteous accents
for his master's life; when he hears in reply their cutting words and
taunting laughter, and hurling the accursed silver at their feet rushes
forth, shrieking that he and they will go down together in the deepest
hell, — the effect produced is overpowering.

A shudder of horror passes over the entire audience, which is

REMORSE OF JUDAS.

only intensified when we see the wretched man wandering over the
open country and crying out in anguish, "For me there is no for-
giveness, no salvation!   I am the outcast villain who hath brought
my benefactor to these bonds and death.   There is no help for me!
For me no hope!   Too late, too late! — for he is dead, and I — I am
his murderer!"

Then, finally, in desperation he loosens his girdle, ties one end about his neck, and prepares to hang himself; the curtain falling at the precise moment when he is fastening the other portion of the girdle to the tree.

Now, the Passion Play continues from eight o'clock in the morning until half past five in the evening, with an intermission of an hour and a half at noon. Let us avail ourselves of this interval to relieve our minds from the continued contemplation of the drama, by looking for a moment on the face of Joseph Maier, while I recall some personal reminiscences connected with him. Through the special introduction of a mutual friend who lodged at his house, I was enabled to see much of him and to converse with him in private. His face, although it cannot be called handsome, lights up in conversation with a most agreeable smile, while his voice is singularly sweet and gentle. His complexion is very pale, and his long, jet-black hair and beard make this pallor the more noticeable.

His features lack something of the sweetness which we associate with the countenance of Jesus; yet their worn and haggard look is, after all, not wholly unsuited to one who could say of himself that he had not where to lay his head. If persistent flattery from the outside world could spoil such a man as Joseph Maier, then would he assuredly be spoiled. Crowds have beset his house and sometimes forced themselves into the retirement of his private

JOSEPH MAIER.

room, merely to rudely stare at him. All this is most offensive to him, and more than once I have seen him look at such intruders like a stag at bay.

"If," he once said, "we country people should go into the city and act there as thousands of these strangers do here, to what ridicule should we not be justly exposed!"

But Maier has more subtle flattery than this. Letters have continuously poured in upon him, expressing in various languages the most lavish adulation. The contents of only one of these was I permitted to know. It was from a distinguished actor in Munich, who assured the peasant of Ober-Ammergau that the hour when he took his arm and walked with him through his mountain village was one of the proudest of his life. It is said (and it is not improbable) that Maier has sometimes had to seclude himself after the Play, to avoid being almost worshipped by some of the Bavarian peasants who have come that day to well-nigh identify him with Christ himself.

Yet I can truly say that I never saw a man more unaffectedly modest and simple than Joseph Maier. The secret is, that he is *thoroughly sincere*. There is no doubt of this. It is not only the greatest conceivable *honor* of his life to represent the character of Jesus, it is also *the most solemn of all religious duties;* and this exalted thought keeps him above the taint of vanity.

I was astonished and pained to see not long ago, in the columns of a New York paper, the statement that most of the people of that city who went to see the Ober-Ammergau Passion Play of 1880 discovered there no sign of reverence in the parts presented, and were more struck by the capacity of Maier to absorb beer, than by his sacred aspirations.

This statement seems to me incredible. I neither believe that the people of New York were so lacking in ability to discover simple piety and intrinsic merit, nor do I credit them with slurring thus the private character of Joseph Maier. That he may drink beer is very probable. He would not be a German, if he did not do so. But that he is (as this would imply) a coarse, sensual man, I pronounce unqualifiedly false. And I do this, not as a defender of religion, nor as a Catholic or Protestant, but simply as a man who hears a worthy person slandered in his absence. I think I may say this the more positively, not only from what I saw of Herr Maier myself, but from the fact that a literary friend of mine who lodged nearly the whole summer at his house, and is certainly qualified to judge of his private life, represents him as a thoroughly refined, modest, sensitive man; pure and blameless in life, unselfish, and devoted to his family.

Even without this testimony of a member of his household, I should not easily doubt the correctness of the estimate which I myself had made of Maier; but with it, I do not hesitate to pronounce the article in question grossly unjust to a sincere and noble-hearted man.

One picture of him I can never forget. It was on Sunday evening, just after the conclusion of the Passion Play. As I was walking through the village I passed his house, and saw his little children run from the door to meet their father, who was returning from the theatre in his ordinary dress. I can see him now, catching them up and holding them to his breast, while his wife looked on from the doorstep with a happy smile!

She, it is said, never attends the Passion Play. She goes sometimes as far as the enclosure, and hears the shouts of exultation as the Christ makes his entry into the Holy City. But she retires then to her own house, unable to behold the terrible scenes of suffering and death which await her husband on the stage, and which there seem so real and vivid as to thrill the heart of even a stranger from beyond the sea.

But after this intermission, resuming our seats once more in the theatre, we first look upon the judgment-hall of Caiaphas, whither Maier has been conducted by the soldiers.

The High-Priest trembles with hatred and rage, as the prisoner is brought before him, exclaiming angrily, " Bring him nearer, that I may look upon his face." Finally, after hearing the testimony of several witnesses, he cries impetuously, " I, the High-Priest, adjure thee by the living God, — tell us, art thou the Messias, the Son of God ? " Maier remains for a moment silent; then with calm dignity makes answer: " Thou hast said; and hereafter shall ye see the Son of Man coming in the clouds of heaven." At these words Caiaphas leaps from his seat, and tearing open the breast of his tunic exclaims, "What need have we of further witnesses? You have all heard his blasphemy. What think ye?" The answer comes at once from all, unanimous and strong: "He is guilty of death!"

CAIAPHAS.

Caiaphas is evidently rejoiced at this verdict, but is conscious that only a partial victory is yet gained. For since Judæa is a Roman province, the sentence must be ratified by the Roman governor, Pilate, to whom the victim is now led.

Thomas Rendl, in his rendition of the rôle of Pilate, unquestionably ranks next to Maier and the Judas in ability. For some time, indeed, the village committee was undecided whether the part of Christ should be given to him or to Joseph Maier. The allotment made, however, was entirely satisfactory; for throughout his entire rôle Pilate bears himself with a dignity worthy of a Roman. His entry on the scene is particularly striking. The stage is largely covered with priests and people, clamoring like hungry wolves for the death of the false prophet and impostor. Attended by one or two officers, Pilate steps calmly forth upon his balcony, and in a cold, impartial voice, which contrasts finely with the howling of the mob, inquires the meaning of the uproar. It is admirable to see his evident disdain for the prejudiced, fanatical priests, as he replies to their accusations, "No *Roman* condemns a man unheard. Let him approach!" The scene between the Christ and Pilate was to me one of the most interesting in the entire drama. The Roman evidently regards him as an innocent and unoffending dreamer. But when Maier utters the words, "My kingdom is not of this world. To this end was I born, and for this cause came I into the world, that I might bear witness to the truth," Pilate looks at him suddenly, as though there flashed upon his mind the possibility of something deeper in the prisoner's thoughts than he had yet believed; and, gazing at him keenly, he utters that well known phrase (echoed, alas! throughout the ages by all thoughtful men), "Was ist Wahrheit?" "What is truth?"

While Pilate is thus hesitating, a servant arrives in haste, bearing a message from his wife, which he begs to deliver immediately.

With all the eagerness of affection, Pilate bids him approach. "What word dost thou bring from my beloved wife?" he asks at once. The servant answers, "She begs of thee most earnestly to have nothing to do with the just man now standing at thy judgment seat, for she has suffered many things in a dream because of him." Pilate makes a gesture as though this confirmed his secret feelings. "Return," he replies quickly, "and tell her she need not fear on this account. I will do all in my power to release him." Then turning to the priests he asks, "Did you not say he was from Galilee?" "Yes," is the reply of many voices; "he comes from Nazareth. He is a Nazarene." "In that case,"

PILATE.

exclaims Pilate joyfully, "this is not my affair. Herod has come from Galilee to Jerusalem to celebrate the feast. Conduct the prisoner, therefore, to his proper judge." With these words he retires; while the priests, furious at this new delay, are forced to conduct their victim to a new tribunal.

Let us follow in his footsteps to where we see a portion of the judgment-hall of Herod, with Maier standing on the extreme right.

JESUS BEFORE HEROD.

Surrounded by his court and a few Jewish priests still trembling
with rage, we see upon the throne the fat, sated voluptuary, who
desires only to be amused. Pilate, notwithstanding his weakness,
inspired us with some respect; but Herod fills us only with disgust.
He evidently looks on Jesus as demented, and wishes to have sport
at his expense. To all his jests, however, Maier returns not a word
in answer, but stands in statue-like repose, as though merely an ape
were chattering before him. Herod at last becomes enraged, and
orders him to be clad in a royal robe, and exhibited to the people as
a king; and when the priests clamor for a judgment he replies,
" My judgment is that he is a fool, and incapable of committing the
crimes which you have laid to his charge." Then, declaring the
council ended, he exclaims to his courtiers, " Come! let us make up
for this lost time with wine and song!"

Again, therefore, Maier is led back to Pilate, who once more
appears upon his balcony. Only a portion of the multitude is here
portrayed, but it is in reality very large and turbulent. The Roman
sees at once that Jesus is the victim of an unreasonable and infu-

riated mob! All now depends upon his firmness. He evidently cannot bear to condemn him, rightly regarding it as a mean and cowardly act. He therefore adopts another plan of rescue, by ordering the thief Barabbas to be brought before him from his dungeon.

With an imperious gesture, he orders the two prisoners to stand thus side by side beneath his balcony. He smiles with satisfaction as he surveys the contrast, confident that he has gained the victory. He might well do so. Can you imagine anything more detestable than this grisly old man, who seems half idiotic as he shuffles out from prison, clad in a greasy gown?

Pilate points to him significantly, and exclaims, as though putting an argument, which must prove conclusive, " Look ye upon these two, and choose which of them, according to custom, I shall at this time release to you." Immediately five hundred hoarse voices cry, again and again, in a tone which chills our blood, " Not this man, but Barabbas! Jesus to the cross! Crucify him! Crucify him!"

CHRIST AND BARABBAS BEFORE PILATE.

Pilate stands for a moment in dumb amazement. Then he turns and looks in pity on the man whom they are thus relentlessly hounding unto death. The cry grows louder, " If thou condemnest not this would-be king, thou art not Cæsar's friend." The one weak point is reached. The Roman governor hesitates and yields; yet, as he does so, he breaks his sceptre, exclaiming in disgust, " Such a people as this I cannot comprehend." Then, as if terrified at what he had done, he calls for water and washes his hands before the multitude, exclaiming fiercely, " Bear me witness! bear me witness! *I* find no fault in him. I wash my hands of his innocent blood." Scarcely

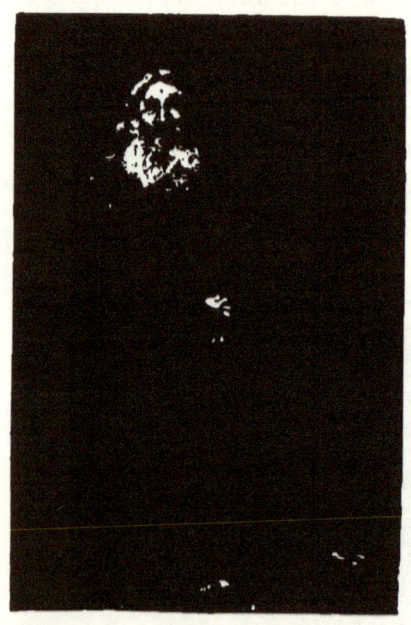

BARABBAS.

have these words fallen from his lips, when the Jews cry out again, in tones that echo over the adjoining hills, "His blood be on us and on our children!"

From this point on, the tragic scenes grow more and more intense. Let us look, for example, upon the spectacle of the scourging. The curtain rises, and reveals upon the central stage the graceful form of Maier bound to a column. His garments are already stained with blood, and amid rude mockery the soldiers are beating him with ropes, the blows from which sound real and terrible. Yet not a groan escapes the sufferer's lips. With a look of agony upon his face he stands there patiently enduring all, until at last his strength can bear no more. He reels. They loosen the rope, and he falls senseless to the ground. But even this is not enough; for, no sooner has he recovered consciousness than the soldiers resume their brutal sport. They place a sceptre in his hands; they seat him on a stool which they call a throne, bowing before him, and doing reverence with vulgar jests. Yes, more than this; they blindfold his eyes and strike him on the face, saying, "Prophesy, O King, who thy next assailant will be!" Finally, they go so far as to push him headlong off the stool, and he falls forward on the floor.

THE SCOURGING.

All this is certainly gross and brutal; yet perhaps it does not exceed the facts of history. Through it all, however, we must bear in mind that Maier never sacrifices for a moment his kingly dignity. All the abuse of his persecutors recoils upon themselves; and we lose not a particle of our admiration for the noble man who never stoops to make complaint, but bears it all with silent heroism.

Finally, however, the climax of their treatment is reached when one of them proposes to add to his regal appearance by crowning the sufferer with thorns! The crown is quickly plaited, and amid brutal exultation is placed upon his pallid brow.

Then, in order not to wound their own hands, four of them take hold of sticks and mercilessly press the thorns down into the bleeding flesh. At this moment there is not a man in the audience who does

not long to leap upon the stage and rescue Maier from such out-
rageous torture; while the excited, breathless look upon the peasants'
faces indicates how deeply they are moved by all this realism.

THE CROWN OF THORNS.

One of the most impressive scenes in the great tragedy is that
which represents the multitude accompanying Jesus to his crucifixion.   It is most imposing; for the crowd numbers hundreds of
people.   Among them is the Roman Centurion on horseback, before
whom is borne a standard with the inscription, "S. P. Q. R." (*Senatus
Populusque Romanus*).   Most of the multitude are filling the air with
taunts and jeering cries; and in their midst we see at length the
doomed man moving slowly, staggering at every step, and dragging
his heavy cross, beneath which he seems at every moment about to
fall.   As he passes one of the houses on the right, there is enacted
the legend of the wandering Jew.   A man appears at the doorway
and bids the Christ be gone, and not disgrace his house by lingering before it.   Maier raises his weary head and fixes on the man
one piercing look.   It is enough.   The haunted wretch turns and
disappears, to find (according to the legend) no rest hereafter upon
earth, — not even that of the grave.

The procession meantime draws slowly nearer to Calvary. The attention of the audience, which has never flagged through all these hours, now becomes almost painfully intensified. For the movement of the cortège is very slow, owing to the extreme weakness of the condemned, who at last, utterly exhausted, wavers, and, borne down by the cross, falls twice heavily to the ground. On each occasion, however, he is goaded up and onward by the soldiers, who have no mercy on his weakness. The Roman Centurion alone seems more humane. He offers him a flagon of water, saying kindly, "Here, refresh thyself." The weary sufferer drinks, and attempts to rise, but cannot do so. A number of the women of Jerusalem stand near him at this moment, weeping at his fate. Maier turns his face toward them, exclaiming with courageous firmness, "Daughters of Jerusalem, weep not for me, but rather for yourselves and for your children!" Among them is the legendary Veronica, who offers him her handkerchief to wipe his brow. Maier takes it, presses it to his face, and returns it to the weeping woman with his blessing. "Remove these women!" orders the Centurion. The soldiers promptly obey, and rudely thrust them aside, while the procession passes slowly on.

Meanwhile, down the street, at the left of the stage, have been advancing Mary the mother of Jesus, Mary Magdalene, and the disciple John. They do not know yet of the condemnation of Jesus, until, alarmed by their own fears and the increasing tumult, they approach the procession. A thrilling moment ensues when Mary recognizes in the suffering man — her son! With a piercing cry

ON THE WAY TO CALVARY.

she falls into the arms of Mary Magdalene, exclaiming in anguish, "Oh, my God! it is my son, — my Jesus!"

A few moments later, when the procession has disappeared, and while the chorus (this time robed in black) are singing their sad chant, we hear behind the curtain the heavy blows of a hammer, and shudder at the thought of the scene which these ominous sounds

THE CRUCIFIXION.

foretell. Another moment, and the curtain rises to reveal to us the scene of Calvary. The crosses of the two thieves are erect on either side, with the malefactors simply bound to them by ropes, no pretence being made in their case of crucifixion. In the centre, the cross of Jesus is at first prostrate. The soldiers are on the point of lifting it; but there is an instant's delay, for the priests have read the title sent by Pilate to decorate the cross, and are enraged at it. They will not have it so, and have sent the messenger back to the Roman governor, insisting that the inscription shall not read, "This is Jesus, the King of the Jews," but rather, "*He said*, I am the King of the Jews." Pilate, however, returns the paper with his well-known words: "What I have written, I have written." As if rejoicing to outwit the priests, the Roman centurion then seizes the paper, and, with one blow from the hammer, nails it just above the sufferer's head.

As the cross was slowly raised to the perpendicular, and Maier was seen suspended thus upon it, I caught my breath, in fearful dread lest it should fall forward and precipitate him to the ground; for he apparently had no support whatever. Not a trace of any ligament could be discerned, and it was hard to believe that he was not actually nailed to the cross.

Let me at once explain this illusion. Maier wears beneath his tightly fitting suit of silk a strong corset, into the back of which are fastened iron rings, which clasp into corresponding rings in the body of the cross. These constitute his only real support; although a very tiny piece of wood is placed beneath one heel, and the nails driven between his fingers give the slightest possible relief to his extended arms. At best, however, to hang there as he does for twenty minutes is, as he himself assured me, exceedingly exhausting. The realism in all this is terrible. Apparently we see the blood-stained nails piercing both hands and feet. The crown of thorns still wounds his forehead; his garments are still marked with the blood of the scourging; and, most trying of all, when the centurion's spear pierces his side, the point enters a little sac concealed beneath his flesh-colored tunic, and actual blood spurts forth!

The figure of Maier, as it hangs upon the cross, is remarkably beautiful and impressive. In a mere physical point of view, it is completely satisfactory. Maier is a man more than six feet tall, and has a form that a sculptor might covet for a model. As he hangs thus upon the cross, relieved against the dark background of the inner stage, I can truly say that I have never seen a crucifix in

IT IS FINISHED.

marble, ivory, or painting, which seemed to me more beautiful.

His words also, uttered from this position, are spoken with inimitable tenderness. Never shall I forget the first sentence which he spoke. Our nerves had been strained to their utmost tension by his previous sufferings and present pitiful position, when we heard him, in a voice broken with pain, answer the railings of the mocking crowd below him with the words: " Father, forgive them ; they know not what they do !"

Soon after, he turns his weary eyes from his mother to the beloved disciple, and exclaims, with indescribable pathos, "Mutter, siehe Deinen Sohn! Sohn, siehe Deine Mutter!"

All the details are carried out just as narrated in the Gospels. The soldiers cast lots for his garments. The sponge is held to his parched lips; and the mysterious, awful words are uttered: " My God, my God, why hast thou forsaken me?" But, finally, it is evident that the end draws near. With a loud voice he cries at last: " Father, into thy hands I commend my spirit."

His head droops wearily upon his breast.

It is finished !

.   .   .   .

The descent from the cross is now enacted. Two ladders are placed against the cross, one in front, the other in the rear. Nicodemus ascends the ladder in the rear, and tenderly draws out the nails from the hands. The arms are then gently laid upon the shoulders of Joseph of Arimathea, who is on the ladder before the cross. Then, by means of a roll of linen cloth, the body is gradually lowered to the ground. Nicodemus, Joseph, and John then lift the body with loving touch, and, with a perfection of skill and tender reverence, lay it at Mary's feet, the head resting on her lap.

What particularly enhanced the pathos of this and other tragic

THE DESCENT FROM THE CROSS.

scenes, was the fact that they occurred thus under the open sky, as if in actual life. The lights and shadows of the clouds fall on the form of Jesus hanging on the cross; the breeze stirs the mantle of his weeping mother; the birds flit lightly back and forth above the stage, as they perhaps once did on Calvary itself, blithely unconscious, now as then, of human tragedy and woe.

One other scene of the Passion Play remains to be considered, — that of the Resurrection. Like all the rest, it is admirably managed. The central curtain rises and reveals the Roman guards watching before the tomb of Jesus. At first they speak of the awful phenomena attendant on the crucifixion; but finally they fall asleep, and all is still. Suddenly a crash as of a thunder-peal is heard. The door of the sepulchre falls prostrate, and for an instant Maier is seen within the doorway clad in a glittering mantle, and with a look of

THE RESURRECTION.

triumph on his pallid face. The next moment two gilded gates spring from the tomb on either side, and meet before him as a dazzling screen of light. Another instant, and they are once more thrown back. But the Christ is gone. We have beheld the vision of the Resurrection.

.   .   .   .

The Passion Play was ended. The last visitor had left the theatre. The curtain of the night had fallen on the earth. No sound was audible within the valley. The stars looked down upon the peaceful

village and on the uncovered stage, where through the day the awful
history of the Son of Man had been again rehearsed with an em-
phasis and pathos whose power and influence were overwhelming.

As I walked thoughtfully that evening through the quiet town,
realizing that on the morrow I was to turn away forever from its
peaceful valley to mingle once more with the outer world, I could
but feel that, among all the thousands gathered there that day, —
however various might have been their individual beliefs concerning
the great Teacher whose life had been so forcibly portrayed, — happily, difference in creed had not implied a lack of reverence or appreciation. No, if our souls are responsive to all that is divinely great
and pure in every form of faith, we can easily find ourselves in sympathy with those who see in this sacred drama a form of their
religion, cherished through generations as a precious privilege, and
hallowed by centuries of historical associations. And having once
attained this sympathy, I venture to affirm that, though thousands
of miles removed from Ober-Ammergau, the memory of this idyllic
hamlet on the heights, and of the drama there enacted, will constantly recur to us, as though some Spirit from a better world were
breathing on our souls its benediction.

PETER THE GREAT

ST. PETERSBURG

THE CITIES OF THE CZAR.

I.

ST. PETERSBURG.

EVEN in these well-regulated days of trains and telegraphs, a journey to Russia offers to the traveller that element of mystery and fascination, which few countries are now fortunate enough to possess. The enormity of its area, its incomprehensible language, its immense railway distances, the ceaseless espionage of its secret police, the deeds of violence within its borders, — all these invest a journey to the country of the Czar with a kind of dread and difficulty, beside which a trip to any other part of Europe seems a mere bagatelle. For Russia is still a country of most violent extremes; a land of splendor and of barbarism, of lavish wealth and utter poverty; a land the rigor of whose frightful climate conquered the otherwise invincible Napoleon and snapped with its keen frosts the pillars of his throne; a land where millions tremble at the breath of one, whose will is fettered by no constitution; a land whose prison is that Siberian realm of ice, whither so many long trains of wretched captives have passed to linger hopelessly in living tombs; a land whose smouldering fires of discontent and hatred, fanned by the ardent breath of Nihilism, are constantly breaking out into rebellion and assassination.

Such were the thoughts which very naturally occurred to us, as we drove through the brilliant streets of Berlin to take the midnight train for St. Petersburg. Our passports had been duly examined and *viséd* by the Russian consul. Our German gold had metamorphosed itself into roubles and copecks. In a few moments we should start for the capital of the Czar of all the Russias. What an excitement always attends one's departure for a strange land! How many half-forgotten pages relating to its character and history, how many legends of its people, how many pictures of its cities, throng confusedly upon the mind, as one really sets out upon his journey thither! Thus all sorts of curious souvenirs occurred to each of us about the land we were to visit. One spoke of the novels of the great Russian romancer, Tourgueneff, and recalled incidents in his "King Lear of the Steppes;" another shuddered at the recollection of tales of Siberian sufferings; a third spoke of "The Exiles," the drama which was recently so successful in Boston; while another opportunely remembered a story read in childhood, of wolves pursuing travellers across the Russian fields. At once the old familiar picture recurred to all of us, of the terrified horses, the reeling sleigh, the mother clasping her children in her arms, and the father preparing even to throw one of his little ones to the howling wolves to stop them in their wild career! These were some of the old reminiscences suggested to us on a murky July night, as we rode beneath a sullen sky to the Eastern station of Berlin.

An arduous undertaking has usually the compensation of special efforts made to reduce its difficulty to a minimum. Thus upon this long route we found sleeping-cars; a luxury so rare in Europe that we fully appreciated their comforts, which moreover reminded us of home. In some respects these foreign sleeping-cars differ from our own. They are considerably wider, and the aisle, instead of extending along the centre, passes down the side of the car. Out of this corridor (lined with windows) doors open into little staterooms, some arranged for two, others for four beds. In the daytime these berths are transformed into sofas, and a pretty table is made to take the place of what appeared the night before to be only a flight of steps. The cost of these luxuries, however, is much more than in America.

A description of our journey through northeastern Prussia would be uninteresting. We passed the time in sleeping, whist-playing and reading ; or if we looked out of the windows we beheld a long succession of cheerless fields, dotted here and there with melancholy windmills, and interrupted only at rare intervals by towns whose principal building seemed to be the railroad station. Only once or twice a city, like Königsberg, or a noble bridge, like that which spans the Vistula, broke the monotony of the scenery. At last, about four o'clock in the afternoon (sixteen hours from Berlin), we halted at the last German town and prepared to cross the frontier.

Nothing else in life is quite like the sensation which the traveller experiences when he stands for the first time upon the threshold of an unknown land. Just two months before, we had passed with beating hearts within the portals of the Pyrenees and sought admission to the country of the Moors. Now we were setting our faces in exactly the opposite direction, and thousands of miles away were craving entrance to the kingdom of the Czar. Here, however, no river, as in Spain, trailed like a silver cord between the two great empires. No mountains reared here, as in southern France, their mighty bulwarks of defence. We could discover no line of demarcation whatever. Yet "there was a time, we knew not when, — a place, we knew not where," that sealed our destinies as Russian tourists; for in a few moments our locomotive had drawn us noiselessly and swiftly from the realm of Kaiser Wilhelm to that of the Czar Alexander, and we had set foot upon the soil of Russia.

The first person whom we encountered on descending from the car was, as we had expected, a police officer, who demanded our passports. Delivering these to him, we followed our baggage into a large hall and waited patiently for half an hour, while a group of officials scrutinized our passports, as though they were holding a council of war. At first my sympathy was excited in behalf of these men, so incessantly did they appear to be hawking, coughing, sneezing and expectorating. After a little time, however, I discovered that these sounds were caused by the simple utterance of the Russian language. If you think this is an exaggeration, try to pronounce a few of the easiest Russian words and see if your friends do not believe that you are suffering from "hay fever." Here are a few for practice :

Schtchí (soup); *Potchámpt* (post-office); *Hórosho* (very well); *Spitchki* (matches); *Gornítchnaya* (chamber-maid); *Ptitsa* (bird).

We had been so frequently told that at all the Russian stations French and German were spoken, that we had not anticipated the slightest difficulty. Of course, both of these languages did serve us many a good turn, but there were times when nothing but the unadulterated, influenza-like Russian was of any avail, and we had to resort to the most comical signs and grimaces. For example, after being released from the Custom House, we prepared to enter our first Russian train. Having tickets for a sleeping-car, we sought to find it. I addressed several officials in French and German; but the replies thus elicited were so unearthly that I gave it up, and selected the best-looking car at a venture. Do you ask why we did not read its name or consult the guide-boards to help us out of our difficulties? But did you ever see the Russian text? Let us have a specimen of it outlined before us.

IV. *Отъ императорскаго александровскаго университета въ Гельсингфорсъ.*

Императорскій александровскій университетъ въ Гельсингфорсѣ, какъ высшій представитель умственной жизни Великаго Княжества Финляндскаго, относясь съ живѣйшимъ участіемъ къ торжеству представителей духовной жизни всей Россіи, чествующихъ нынѣ въ Москвѣ свѣтлую память великаго русскаго поэта, Александра Сергѣевича Пушкина, поручилъ одному изъ своихъ заслуженныхъ профессоровъ, Степану Ивановичу.

It is very pretty to look at, as a set of hieroglyphics, but hardly what one would choose for light reading when in the hurry of travel! Those recipes for sneezing which I cited a moment ago become still more fearful when consolidated into Russian type. Take two dozen of our letters, turn them upside-down or backwards, make monograms of them, sprinkle in a few figures, add as many Greek characters, and then elongate them hap-hazard into words of various dimensions, and you will have some idea of the Russian alphabet, as it appears to the naked eye of one not versed in its mysteries. Giving up the language therefore, as a hopeless task, let us turn our attention to the route between the frontier and St. Petersburg. At one place our train stopped at Kovno on the river Niemen, where the grand army of France, on the 23d of June, 1812, crossed the stream on their advance to Moscow; and some rising ground near by is still called "*Napoleon's Hill.*" Six months later, the French recrossed this river in the same place, after sufferings which have had no parallel in the annals of war. In the market-place of the town is a monument with this inscription: "In 1812 Russia was invaded by an army numbering seven hundred thousand men. The army recrossed the frontier numbering seventy thousand!" Another halting-place was Wilna, whose population even as late as the fourteenth century was pagan, and where, less than four hundred and fifty years ago, a perpetual fire was kept burning to the honor of the heathen gods. It was at Wilna that Napoleon left his retreating army and hastened on to Paris to quiet there a threatened insurrection. Twenty thousand wounded and half-frozen Frenchmen were found here by the pursuing Russians, and in one hospital alone Alexander beheld seven thousand, five hundred dead bodies piled one above the other! How horrible are the calamities of war!

Although it was after midnight when we passed this city, yet it was not dark. At two o'clock in the morning, I could read a letter perfectly without the aid of artificial light. Only a short time before, we had watched the sun set in splendor. In two hours it would rise again. Truly, in summer, the god of day seems to be troubled with insomnia in Russia!

As this prolonged twilight is not conducive to our own slumbers, let us step out upon the station platform. There is plenty of time. Russian trains go slowly, and make long stops. Moreover, there is no danger of being left, for three warning bells are always sounded preparatory to the start. Here, as at most stations, is a large refreshment room. We naturally direct our steps thither, for the keen night air of Russia gives us an appetite.

On entering we see a characteristic Russian sight, which the traveller will never forget. Besides the usual display of viands which might be found in any railway restaurant in Europe, we behold here a peculiarity of Russia. Upon a long table are perhaps one hundred glass tumblers, each containing two lumps of sugar and a spoon. Beside each glass also is a slice of lemon. Any one but a resident of Maine would instantly suspect from these indications the formation of a whiskey punch; for behind these suspicious-looking

RUSSIAN TEA-DRINKERS.

glasses stand several persons, pouring alternately from two pitchers something which, when combined, glows with the color of a dark ruby. All our fellow-passengers hasten at once to enjoy this Russian nectar. In fact, Russian trains move slowly and make long stops for the special purpose, I verily believe, of allowing both passengers and officials to refresh themselves with this great national drink of Russia, namely, *Tea*.

But what tea! Not such as even the best American merchants sell; not such as any of my untravelled readers have ever tasted; for, boast of your oolong and your souchong as much as you like, vaunt to the skies the English breakfast tea which Bridget makes for you every morning, you have no idea how truly *delicious* tea can be, until you come to Russia! Is it in its preparation that it acquires such an exquisite flavor, or is the secret in the tea itself? The Russians, of course, say the latter, and add that, as their tea is brought overland from China, it has a much more delicate taste than that which is conveyed to other parts of the world by sea. The preparation, indeed, seems simple enough. A large urn, called the *samovar*, contains the precious liquid, which is kept continually heated by gas-jets beneath. When it is served, about two tablespoonfuls are poured into the tumbler, to which is added three times as much hot water. A slice of lemon is then launched upon its surface, and the nectar is ready to be imbibed. If it be objected that the tea is boiling hot, I cannot deny that for a few moments this fact detracts from the pleasure of the tea-drinker; but it is an inconvenience which quickly disappears, and can hardly, indeed, be reckoned as a fault when the long Russian winter returns from its brief leave of absence.

Russia has its blemishes, as we shall hereafter see. Russia has discomforts, annoyances, dirt, beggars, ignorance and vice. But it possesses two things which cover a multitude of sins, and the memory of which will long outlast even that of the bite of Moscow fleas, — namely, Russian *bread*, and above all Russian TEA! In fact, the Russian word *Tchai* (Tea) is a most important one for the traveller to the land of the Czar to learn at the very start, not only that he may ask for the precious beverage himself, but because when Russian coachmen or servants solicit a fee, instead of the *Pourboire* of the French, the *Buona mano* of the Italians, the *Trinkgeld* of Germany and the *Backsheesh* of the Orient, we shall hear only the magic words, "*Na tchai*," — "*For tea!*"

It is now seven o'clock in the afternoon, and we shall soon be in St. Petersburg; yet the scenery is unchanged. Through dreary, uncultivated wastes we have ridden all day long; but, since there are no distinguishing features in the landscape, we might fancy ourselves just where we were twelve hours ago. Amid these desolate wilds and stunted forests, within an hour's ride of the Czar's capital, bears, elk and wolves are yearly killed in large numbers. A fine place Russia would be for a train to break down in some winter night, when the mercury marked thirty degrees below zero, and the wolves wanted a free ride! But accidents do not often happen on Russian railroads. Perhaps when we send our careless railroad managers to cool off in Alaska after a mishap, we also shall travel in security. But at length there comes an end to the monotony of the journey, and we suddenly behold rising before us, like some strange exhalation from the deep, St. Petersburg, the famous city of the Czar! In amazement then at the contrast between these stately

ST. PETERSBURG.

buildings and the desolate land through which we have been travelling, we naturally ask ourselves, How was it that a city ever came
to be built in so strange a spot as this, hardly above the level of the
sea, and almost within the Arctic Circle?

Have you ever seen the Russian coat of arms? If so, you remember the immense double-headed eagle of Russia, one head turned

toward Asia, and the other toward Europe. Peter the Great (the most remarkable of the Russian Czars) desired to have in his kingdom what he called "a window through which this Russian eagle could look out into civilized Europe." In 1703, therefore, he selected this site on the marshy banks of the river Neva, and there laid the foundation of the enormous city now called by his name. It was a fearful undertaking, a prodigious struggle against nature; but Peter was not a man to recoil before difficulties. Moreover, a despot may do as he pleases. Were laborers needed? He caused an immense number of Russians, Tartars, Cossacks and Finns to come and build his capital. But laboring in the cold and wet, without suitable food or shelter, multitudes yielded to the hardships; and it is said that the foundations of St. Petersburg were laid at a cost of one hundred thousand lives in the first six months! Yet this ought not to surprise us, when we think that even now St. Petersburg is so unhealthful a place that during the last twelve years the deaths there have outnumbered the births by more than twenty thousand; and, were it not for the constant accessions from the country, its present population would be soon extinguished! Were citizens needed? A nod from Peter, and they came fast enough; for, if a nobleman built a house for himself anywhere else in Russia, he must also erect one in St. Petersburg, or else probably inhabit one in Siberia. Thus, this great city of St. Petersburg, in one respect, resembles the Pyramids, since it is a magnificent monument of autocratic power.

Meanwhile Peter himself, the moving spirit of the whole, superintended the work in person, and dwelt on the banks of the Neva, in the little cottage which every traveller surveys with interest. "But this," you will exclaim, "is not a cottage; it is a church." And you are right; yet so am I; for the original house of Peter, built by his own hands, is contained within it, like a jewel in a box. It stands beneath the second of these domes, and consists of but three apartments, — a bedroom, dining-room and kitchen. These, however, contain many memorials of Peter, the most interesting of which to me was the boat which he himself constructed, and which is therefore called the grandfather of the Russian fleet.

But what a difference between these rooms of Peter then and now! His bedroom, for example, has now been changed into a gorgeous chapel, with alabaster floor and ceiling, and walls which

COTTAGE OF PETER THE GREAT.

gleam with paintings and magnificent gems; for Peter has become a saint, and prayers are addressed to him now from every part of the great empire.

From here it is but a step to the banks of the Neva, which once more spreads before us its unruffled mirror. From the enormous volume of its clear, blue water this is surely one of the noblest rivers in Europe. Yet, two hundred years ago it was almost unknown. For thousands of years it had flowed on through trackless forests, its shores resounding only to the shouts of savage fishermen and hunters. Now it is known the world over as the great commercial artery of Russia, and sweeps along in majesty to cast itself upon the bosom of the Baltic, and murmur with delight of the splendor of this new-born Russian city through which it has cleft its way!

Along its banks are many pretty villas, whither the wealthy Russians betake themselves in summer beyond the precincts of the dusty town ; and often of a summer evening, during that long and fascinating twilight of the North, which constitutes one of the greatest charms of the Czar's capital, I have seen its surface rippled by a multitude of graceful boats, some of which float idly at their moorings like the gondolas of Venice. But let us now turn from the Neva to one of the numerous canals connected with it, which intersect St. Petersburg in various directions. From this we can easily understand the perilous situation of the city. No part of it is more than fifteen feet above the level of the sea, and most of it lies so low that, notwithstanding all the efforts of Peter and his successors for two hundred years, no art can avoid occasional inundations. The very ground seems to tremble under the enormous weight imposed upon it, and the whole city to float unsteadily on the waters, like a vessel loaded down to the water's edge with precious goods. Guns

are always fired from the fortress whenever the river begins to rise, and, when it reaches a certain point, the very frequent discharge of cannon warns the occupants of cellars to seek places of refuge, and the police begin to prepare boats and to insure the safety of men and merchandise. Yet, when one looks upon this city basking in the mellow twilight of its northern summer, who would imagine that it bears within its bosom the

THE NEVA.

elements of its own destruction?　But if a great ocean storm should ever occur in April, when the ice is breaking up in Lake Ladoga (the

A CANAL IN ST. PETERSBURG.

source of the Neva), the news might flash across the Atlantic that a similar catastrophe had happened here to that of 1824, when thirteen hundred houses were destroyed and eight hundred persons drowned; or, in fact, that the city of the Czars had sunk forever into those gloomy marshes over which its sovereignty now seems so complete.

> "Build up your granite piles
> Around my trembling isles,
> I hear the River's scornful Genius cry:
> Raise for eternal time
> Your palaces sublime,
> And flash your golden turrets in the sky.
>
> "But in my waters cold
> A mystery I hold,
> Of empires and of dynasties the fate;
> I bend my haughty will,
> But am unconquered still;
> I smile to note your triumph; *mine* can wait!"

But, notwithstanding its attendant dangers, the breaking up of the ice-bound Neva is always a season of rejoicing in St. Petersburg. A curious ceremony then takes place. The first boat that crosses the liberated river bears the Governor of the fortress to the Winter Palace, where he presents a goblet of Neva water to the Czar. The latter drinks, has the glass emptied, and returns it to the Governor filled to the brim with gold pieces. This pretty custom was at one time almost spoiled, however, through the avarice of the Governor. The Emperor noticed that every year the goblet increased in size, thus necessitating a greater number of gold pieces to replenish it! Accordingly he named a fixed sum to be placed in the glass, irrespective of its capacity, — which, however, is doubtless sufficiently large to recompense the Ganymede of the Neva.

Of course, with such a foundation as St. Petersburg possesses, you may easily imagine it is emphatically a city of *bridges*. Let us, therefore, fancy that our horses' feet are ringing on one of the finest of them all, — the bridge of St. Nicholas. It spans the Neva in a series of iron arches, resting on magnificent granite piers. Beneath it is the noble river, which sweeps along with rapid current, as if rejoicing in its brief freedom from icy fetters; for during the greater part of the year its waters are bridged over by a crystal pavement, on which the heaviest burdens pass in safety, where large ships floated and blue waves tossed perhaps only a fortnight before. The numerous branches of the Neva form then a series of glittering boulevards, into whose shining pavement lamp-posts are placed, and which for months assume all the characteristics of spacious, crowded thoroughfares, locking their white arms tightly about the city of the Czar. Meanwhile you have doubtless noticed near the centre of this bridge a little building. It is a most characteristic Russian sight, namely, a shrine for prayer. I should be afraid to hazard a statement as to the number of such shrines as this in St. Petersburg. Their name is "legion," and before them morning, noon and night there is the same show of devotion. Almost every person who passes over this bridge pauses long enough to cross himself before this chapel of

St. Nicholas. Some even prostrate themselves, and kiss the dirty pavement. Others purchase a candle of a merchant near by, light it, and leave it burning before the picture of the saint in one of these mosaic arches. Thus, in walking through the most crowded streets of St. Petersburg or Moscow, you will suddenly observe a man take off his hat, cross himself repeatedly and perhaps stand still in prayer, before some little shrine, which otherwise would have escaped your notice. After a time one becomes so accustomed to

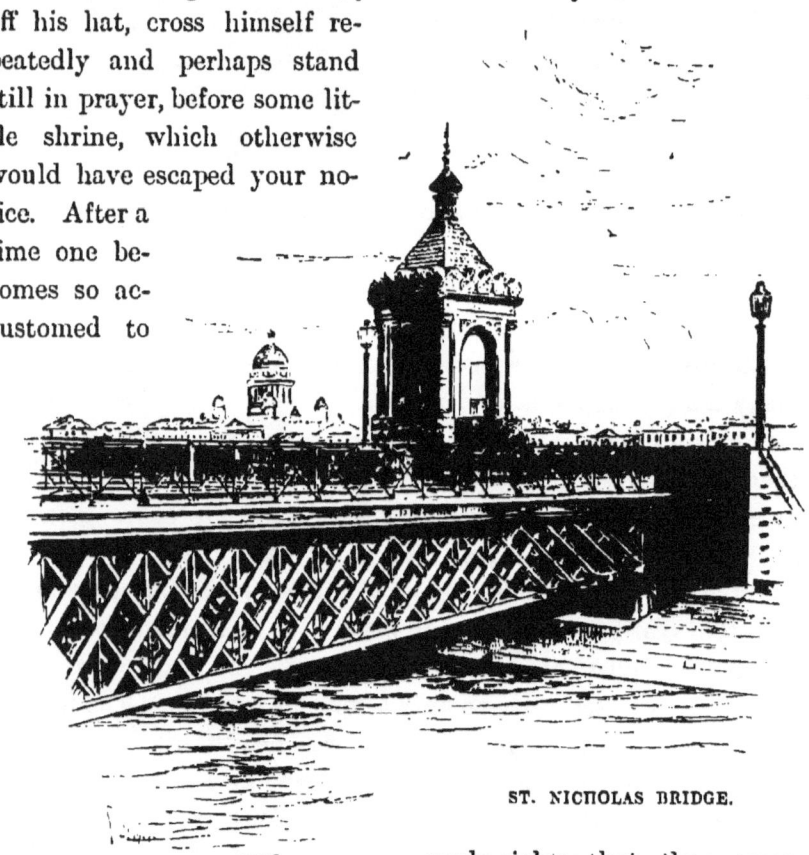

ST. NICHOLAS BRIDGE.

such sights that they cease to strike him with astonishment.

But we ourselves have halted long enough before this chapel to be solicited by the candle-merchant. Making our way, therefore, to the end of this bridge, we shall see before us a spacious building, whose name we instantly inquire. It is the residence of one of the Czar's relatives, and is a fair specimen of the finest mansions in St. Petersburg.

The color of such houses is usually reddish brown or yellow, and this first leads us to suspect that the material of which they are composed is not real stone. " What ! " you exclaim, " are not those Corinthian columns, those elaborate cornices and those sculptured figures carved in stone ? " Prepare yourselves for a disappointment.

A PALATIAL RESIDENCE.

They are only stucco. This matters little, of course, when merely private dwellings are concerned; but unfortunately the same thing is true of most of the palaces and public buildings of St. Petersburg and Moscow. True, they are all of colossal size, like the empire in which they stand. But it will not do to examine them too closely ;

for stone alone gives any value to such ornaments as they possess; and, strange to say, in a land of such mineral wealth, stone work is rare in Russia.

When, therefore, St. Petersburg emerges from its winter frosts, and shakes off its coats of stucco and of ice together, it presents a most forlorn appearance, — like a dilapidated vessel coming into port from a tempestuous voyage. "But are there no exceptions to this order of things?" you ask. Yes, assuredly there are; and to one of them we now gladly turn, namely, St. Isaac's Cathedral.

ST. ISAAC'S CATHEDRAL.

This is an illustration of the fact that when Russia really puts forth the effort, she can and does surpass the modern world in the splendor of her architecture; since the treasures of her quarries are exhaustless, and the skill of her lapidaries unexcelled. It is, however, unfortunate that there is no eminence in the city on which St. Isaac could have been placed; for at this distance it is impossible to see to advantage the magnificent flight of steps leading to its portico. Yet, I assure you, each of these steps is one gigantic block of rose granite, worthy of the Egyptian temple of Karnak. Moreover, the portico itself is supported by stupendous columns of the same material, sixty feet in height, and seven in diameter, and polished like the unbroken surface of a mirror.

" Well," you perhaps exclaim, " what is there so remarkable in this portal to distinguish it from others ? " But look along those columns for their lines of jointure. You will discover none. They are monoliths. Yes, every one of them *one solid mass of beautifully polished stone !* With the exception of Pompey's pillar in Egypt and the Alexander column, — which we shall presently examine, — they are indeed the largest monoliths which the hand of man has ever quarried, turned and polished ! Now, ordinarily, a temple is content with one such portal as this ; but reflect that this magnificence is here repeated on each of the four sides of the edifice.

Moreover, from the centre of the structure the mighty dome rises to the height of two hundred and ninety-six feet, and is itself also surrounded by thirty monolithic shafts ; while the roof, which gleams like a miniature sun, is covered with a mass of gold worth two hundred and fifty thousand dollars. What wonder, then, that the cost of the whole cathedral was more than fourteen millions of dollars ; one million having been expended in merely driving into the soil a perfect forest of piles, to make a sufficiently strong foundation for the enormous mass !

But, if this be the exterior, how shall I describe the interior of this temple of the North ?

Before its gilded altar-screen are ten columns of malachite *thirty feet high*, and columns of lapis-lazuli, each of which cost thirty thousand dollars ! This exceeds every other display of these marvellous stones which the world knows. We are accustomed to regard a small fragment of either of them as a valuable ornament. Imagine then *whole columns of them five times as high as ourselves !* Yet this is only in keeping with the entire building ; for we tread there a pavement of variegated marble ; we ascend steps of polished jasper ; we clasp railings of alabaster ; we are surrounded by walls gleaming with pieces of jasper, verd-antique, porphyry and malachite, cut in various designs and exquisitely polished, interspersed here and there with vast mosaic portraits of the saints, and shrines of gold incrusted with jewels! The whole, in fact, is so magnificent as to seem incredible till actually seen.

But, as I have already said, Russia is a land of violent extremes and startling contrasts. We have just seen some striking archi-

tectural differences. Let us now turn to survey some of the people whom we may encounter on the very steps of St. Isaac's itself. Dear readers, you have doubtless in the course of your lives seen dirty people, — it may be dirty clothing. It is not important to what race or nationality these untidy people have belonged. It is sufficient for my purpose that you now have in mind an ideal of filthy humanity. Yet, no matter how disgusting this ideal may be, I venture to say it falls short of the actual appearance of a common Russian peasant. I myself have seen the beggars of Constantinople, shrunk from the lepers of Jerusalem, laughed at the dirty Neapolitans, held my nose in a Spanish crowd, and gazed pityingly at the wretched fellahs

A RUSSIAN PEASANT.

of Egypt; but, in my opinion, for the concentration and embodiment of all that is dirty and repulsive the common Russian carries off the palm. It is a significant fact that in their own language the name by which these lowest Russians are designated is " *Tschornoi narod*," — the " *Dirty People*." Semi-nakedness is preferable, in an æsthetical point of view, to a Russian peasant's clothes. Let us look upon still another of these barbarians of the North, while I give you what I consider a recipe for making a Russian peasant's dress. Take an old, tattered, blue dressing-gown, which you have worn for ten years, and use it twice as a mop to clean a stable floor; rub wheel-grease into the lower half, and let it dry black and hard in the sun; next sprinkle the upper half with hot lard and candle-drippings, not forgetting to give the sleeves a double quantity; then wipe off a street-crossing with it thoroughly, choosing a particularly muddy day for the trial; next wet it with ill-smelling cabbage-soup (the favorite food of the peasants), and tear several holes in it; finally, let your dog sleep in it for two years; then select for its wearer a man whose beard looks like a bramble-bush, and whose hair has been gashed off behind with a knife and fork; tie it tightly about his waist with an old cloth belt, and on no account let the bearer wear a collar; put on the man's head a cap which resembles a woollen cuspidor; and, finally, encase his feet in dirty rags tied about with strings. Thus only can you have an idea of the appearance of a Russian of the lower class, as I have seen them by the hundreds, and I may say thousands. This costume, however, forms only the *summer* clothing of the peasants. But with the first approach of winter a change is made. Note that I am not rash enough to say that any of their summer clothing is then taken off; on the contrary, I doubt if it be ever removed until dissolved by age or grasped by the grim fingers of the undertaker. But something extra is put on; and what is it? It is a sheep's skin, not such as you obtained on graduating from Harvard or Yale, but a genuine coat made of the skin of defunct mutton. Now, these coats are handed down from father to son for several generations. They are never laid aside during the night, and never washed! Moreover, they are always worn with the wool turned inward; so that the

ONE OF THE "DIRTY PEOPLE."

exterior presents to view the unadorned pelt of the sheep. Even in July I saw scores of these "wolves in sheep's clothing," apparently sweltering under the noon-day sun. "But these," you will say, "are of course only the lowest country people, a few of whom have strayed into the city by accident." Not at all. These dirty, unkempt, repulsive *Moujiks* constitute quite a considerable part of the population of the city. I was more astonished by this than by anything else in Russia. I had imagined that I should see upon the famous Nevski Prospekt elegant carriages, beautiful ladies, elaborate toilettes, Russian dandies and all that display of luxury and wealth which we naturally associate with the principal street in the capital of the Czar. Instead of this, which would have recalled the boulevards of Paris, I saw hundreds of uncombed barbarians, enveloped in the dirty blue gowns which I have attempted to describe, — some returning from work, others sitting about in idleness, and others (a fraction cleaner in appearance) mounted upon little wagons called "droschkies," and angling with their whips for passengers, as eagerly as a fisherman for trout. Well dressed and cleanly persons were decidedly in the minority, and always surprised me by the comparison which their appearance instantly suggested. Unquestionably, had my visit to St. Petersburg been made in winter, rather than in summer, I should have seen there a far greater number of gay equipages, elegant toilettes and cultivated people; since in July and August the wealthy citizens are mostly absent from the capital. But even then the "plebeians" must have far outnumbered the "patricians."

Not many years ago Napoleon said, " Scratch a Russian, and you will find beneath a Tartar." Something of this is doubtless true of the vast majority of the population of Russia to-day. The cultivated Russians, whom we meet in Europe and America, and justly admire for their refinement and culture, are very few ; while the great mass of the people are still but slightly removed from a half-savage state.

But, turning from the people in the city streets, let us look for a moment upon some of the streets themselves. Here what surprised me most was the apparent lack of people to fill them. Compared with the streets of London, Paris or New York, most of these highways of St. Petersburg seem tranquil and deserted. Even in winter, the season of greatest gayety, I fancy the impression would be much the same. The fact is that the Czar's capital is as yet too large for its population. Its buildings are too many and too vast for its inhabitants. Its immense squares and streets seem adapted only for large bodies of troops, and we feel their absence. Indeed, on such a

A STREET IN ST. PETERSBURG.

colossal scale is the city built, that I doubt if its population will ever adequately fill the gigantic frame allotted to it by its arbitrary founder. The scanty foliage along these streets need not surprise us, so near are we now to the cold shoulder of Greenland. But oh, shades of the martyrs, what *pavements* exist in some of these St. Petersburg highways! I suppose that winter furnishes them so good a pavement for more than half the year that in summer people are contented here with almost anything. Twice, in driving through St. Petersburg in the month of July, our carriage was stuck fast in the mud, and we continued our route on foot! So numerous also were the stones and holes, that we often bobbed about in the carriage like kernels of popped corn; while our features twitched as though we had St. Vitus' dance. I remember trying to call out once the Russian word for driver, *Isvotschik*, but the terrific jolts caused me to almost bite my tongue off in the attempt!

And, by the way, let us look for a moment on one of the characteristic Russian cabs in which we rattle over these pavements. A Russian droschky is a genuine curiosity. It has, as you see, four wheels, about as large as that of a wheelbarrow. Upon this a slender framework is raised, containing usually two seats, — a very small one for the driver, and behind this another for the passenger. I use the singular, for the seat is hardly wide enough for two, unless they happen to be situated as were the Siamese twins, and even then the disagreeable proximity of the driver's coat suggests unpleasant zoölogical experiences. This is a comparatively elegant droschky; but oh, what specimens some of them are! "The one-horse shay" in its last moments never looked so badly. Even the wagon which

A RUSSIAN DROSCHKY.

Methuselah had used from his youth up, through all his "nine hundred and ninety-nine" years, never began, I am sure, to have such a desperately seedy air as a second-rate Russian droschky. I did not dare to get into one of that class, for I knew that if I did, I should justly forfeit my life insurance. It is an instrument of torture applied to locomotion. An English nobleman once offered, it is said, a thousand pounds to any one who would find in a civilized country a more uncomfortable vehicle. He has his money still!

By way of recompense, however, the horses which draw even the poorest of these vehicles are by no means such skinny, nerveless beasts as those which we commiserate in Paris and in Naples. Almost without exception, the Russian horses are beautiful. They are small, nimble, elegantly formed and sleek. Their harnesses are so light that they seem to be mere ribbons of leather; while a curious arch extends from one shaft to the other over the horse's head, making the head of the pretty animal appear as if set in a picture-frame. These horses go like the wind. No matter whether you are riding "by the course" or "by the hour," you will be whirled over Peter's paving-stones with a rapidity that startles you. I can account for it only from the fact that during the greater part of the year these horses drag light sleighs over an icy crust, and thus get accustomed to a rapid rate of progress. Delighted, therefore, with this mode of locomotion (so far at least as the horses were concerned), we rode incessantly about the city, finding at every turn sights to amuse, astonish or instruct us.

The great artery of the capital is the "Nevski Prospekt," or "Perspective of the Neva,"—a street one hundred and twenty feet broad, and extending straight as an arrow for a distance of three miles. Among the many objects which embellish it we note the Alexander Theatre, — one of the finest in the city, and adorned with many handsome statues. To the honor of Russia be it said, the Government of the Czar devotes yearly a very large sum of money to the cultivation of dramatic art in all its branches; justly recognizing the drama as a means of popular education and culture, as well as of amusement. Operas are as finely given in Russia as anywhere in the world, the best talent being always engaged, and the stage arrangements leaving nothing to be desired. It is in St. Petersburg, you remember, that Patti, Nilsson, and our own sweet-voiced Cary have won some of their most brilliant triumphs.

Close by this theatre we observe another ornament of the Nevski

Prospekt, namely, the Imperial Library. One would hardly expect the library of so young a nation as Russia to be especially remarkable; but in reality this building contains one of the richest collections in the world. Here are some invaluable documents relating to the history of France, dragged from the archives of Paris at the time of the French Revolution by an infuriated populace, and sold to the first bidder. A Russian purchased them, and thus some of the most valuable state papers of France adorn the library of the Czar. Here too is the famous manuscript of the Gospels discovered by Professor Tischendorf at the lonely monastery of Mt. Sinai, — a work dating from the fourth century, and the oldest and most authentic copy of the Gospels extant. The collection of Hebrew manuscripts here is also the most unique and ancient in the world, far surpassing that of the British Museum or the Imperial Library at Paris.

One of its greatest treasures, however, is an immense Koran, written on gazelle skin. It was purchased some years ago at a mosque in Asia. Tradition says it was the first complete Koran ever written, and was made for the Caliph Osman. It was this volume which was once kept in the magnificent mosque of Cordova, in Spain, and it was this very book that Osman was reading when his murderers attacked him, and upon it are still visible the traces of his blood.

From this let us approach the famous Alexander column, — a monument of which all Russia may be justly proud. It is the greatest monolith of modern times, being a single shaft of red granite, *forty-two feet in circumference,* and *eighty-four feet high,* exclusive of capital and pedestal! This would not have been unworthy of Egypt. When we behold it standing so securely on its pedestal, it is hard to realize the almost incredible amount of labor necessary to bring it from its mountain quarry and erect it here. But, since the whole of St. Petersburg is built upon a morass, it was needful to drive here no less than six rows of piles, one above the other, in order to furnish a strong enough foundation for the enormous burden of *four hundred tons* resting on so small a base. The summit of this

splendid shaft is sur-
mounted by the figure of
an angel, fourteen feet in
height, holding a cross.
This statue was raised
to its present elevation
in its rough state, and
was polished after being
firmly fixed in its posi-
tion. On the pedestal
—which, like the capital,
is ornamented with bronze
— we read the brief but
expressive inscription,
"Grateful Russia to Alex-
ander I." It is said that
the French king Louis
Philippe once coolly asked
the Czar Nicholas for a
similar column out of his
Finland quarries. The

THE ALEXANDER COLUMN.

Czar, however, begged to be excused. "I do not wish," he said, "to
send you a smaller one; a similar one I cannot afford; and a greater
one it is impossible to obtain."

As we turned away from this noble monolith on the night of our
arrival in St. Petersburg, the slowly descending globe of the northern
sun was flooding the city with a marvellous radiance, and gilding
brightly the summit of the column. In fact, so far into the night
did this illumination linger there, clothing the angel and his cross
with glory, that we could almost fancy it unwilling to leave them,
until they should again be greeted by the kiss of dawn.

But no longer let us delay a visit to the celebrated Winter Palace,
—one of the largest buildings in the world, and for the greater part of
the year the residence of the Czar of all the Russias. Seen from a
distance, you can hardly imagine a palace more imposingly designed

and nobly situated; for its dimensions are gigantic, and beside it rolls the Neva, like a flood of silver. In fact, in size and situation, this reminded me not a little of the Sultan's splendid palace on the Bosphorus. Since the assassination of Alexander, and the blowing up by dynamite of the dining-room of this palace, the police have been exploring it from top to bottom. Never was there such a house-cleaning as that has proved to be; for, besides the men-servants and maid-servants, the porters, grooms, soldiers and courtiers,

THE WINTER PALACE.

whose names are all registered on the palace books, there were discovered here numbers of people of whose very existence the police were ignorant. People had come hither with former Czars or their officials, and had forgotten to leave when their masters died, remaining here thus for years, and marrying, and even rearing their families here without special notice. Five or six thousand people at one time are said to have resided in this palace. Startling discoveries were made at every turn, the most ludicrous being the finding of a cow in a shed upon the roof. No one knew how she came there; but she was probably brought thither when quite young, that her milk might be sold to these curious inmates of the palace.

The apartments of Alexander II. were in the second story of this palace, and there of course was centred the Imperial Court. Yet one story higher was another court to which Russian statesmen and courtiers crowded almost as eagerly. For there, above the Czar's apartments, was the splendid suite of rooms occupied by the Princess Dolgorouki, whom for years Alexander loved with passionate devotion. It was only the actual members of the imperial family who looked with jealousy on the fair intruder and dared to keep aloof from the court of the upper story. Of course every one surmised, when the illness of the Empress took a serious turn, that the Czar would soon marry the princess; still it was with great surprise and not a little disgust that, only four months after the death of his first wife, St. Petersburg learned that Alexander had led his second consort to the altar.

Viewed from a distance, this Winter Palace appears noble and majestic, and it would be easy to leave that impression on your minds; for nothing in this illustration betrays the fatal secret of its composition. But I am sure you would rather know facts than be deceived by careless works of travel. One American writer, has stated that it is built of brown stone. Relying on his accuracy, I was again doomed to disappointment. It is really a palace of brick, stuccoed over and painted brown. Worse than that, when I beheld it, the plastering had fallen off and the harsh red brick showed underneath in many places, like an ugly sore. Certainly this palace is admirably designed and of vast proportions; but (save in the one particular of size) its exterior is unworthy of the home of the Emperor of Russia, and is completely wanting in that massive solidity which its name suggests.

But note that I lay especial stress upon the *exterior;* for when we have passed within its painted shell, we find at every turn the most lavish expenditure and gorgeous adornment. At present no travellers in Russia would be allowed to go within this palace; but at the time of my visit to St. Petersburg, it was (in the absence of the Czar) open to all tourists.

I was two hours in passing through its scores of splendid halls; and I assure you it is no easy task to walk over its miles of polished floors and through its endless corridors, where crystal chandeliers, malachite tables, inlaid doors and ornaments innumerable dazzle the eye, and finally become indescribably wearisome and monotonous. Without doubt, to keep this enormous palace in good order must be a great expense to the Government; but it has just come to light that for years there have been "Star-Route" house-cleaners here. For example, fifteen hundred roubles have been charged every year merely for *brooms to sweep it !* But on estimation it is found that at this rate eighteen thousand of these brooms must have been used here yearly, and that nearly fifty must have been worn out every day during the reign of the late Alexander! From this one item we can imagine what other frauds went on within this palace, and can understand the remark of the Czar Nicholas, when he exclaimed, "My son and I are the only ones in Russia who do not steal!"

In one part of this building is a magnificent chapel designed for the use of royalty. In the sanctuary of this we were shown a great number of holy relics, the most remarkable of which was *the hand and a part of the arm of the Virgin Mary !* This relic, kept under a glass case, was a hideous sight; for it was so black and shrivelled with age that it might equally well have been called the paw of an embalmed monkey.

Other relics were a part of the robe of Jesus, and two pictures said to have been painted by St. Luke. It seems that some persons a few centuries ago doubted whether one of these paintings was a genuine production of St. Luke's genius; so the saint was considerate enough to sign it one night, which of course settled the question. My faith in this matter of the signature, however, is lukewarm. With the advanced ideas of art which he must possess, I think Luke would

have been ashamed to sign such a daub. I asked our guide whether
the Czar believed in all these relics. The reply was, "Of course;
why not?"

But now let us pass into the great ball-room of this palace, which
is indeed an apartment of crystallized splendor. It is, I believe, con-

BALL-ROOM, WINTER PALACE.

ceded that no court balls in Europe are so brilliant as those which
are given here. Often one of the larger halls is then converted into
an almost tropical garden by the introduction of exotic plants and
fruit trees; and thus one passes, as if by magic, from the snow-
covered street, and a temperature of thirty degrees below zero, into

the gorgeous splendor of a Southern carnival. There, only a few feet removed from icicles and the glacial blasts of the North, one inhales the perfume of flowers, and feels upon his cheek a warmth soft as the breath of Egypt. But this is not the only room which can be thus adorned; for on entering the elegant breakfast-room of the Czar, we noticed another profusion of Southern plants and flowers. Born amid snow and ice, the Russians have a passion for these emblems of the Orient. The beauty of these rooms must, however, have only heightened the misery of the late Czar during the last years of his life, when he was as much haunted by the fear of murder as is his son to-day. The floor of the neighboring dining-hall was, you remember, blown up by dynamite just as he was about to enter it. Finally his kitchen was placed under strict surveillance, three physicians being attached to it, each of them receiving 1,000 roubles a month. One examined the meats, vegetables and pastry; another tasted the wines and liquors; the third superintended the cooking of the dishes. They were all subject to grave responsibilities. At the least illness of the Czar they ran the risk of being arrested as accomplices, on a charge of high treason, and of being instantly banished to Siberia or put to death. And yet it is said that the Czar, fearing to depend entirely upon those safeguards, frequently took emetics after his meals, as an additional precaution !

Such reflections naturally remind us of some of the attempts made by the Nihilists to enter here.

General Gourko, when governor of St. Petersburg, had the right of entering at any time into the Emperor's room without being announced. Once, however, the guard in one of the ante-rooms, seeing something unusual about his appearance, stopped him, saying that it would be necessary to inform the Czar of his arrival. The general objected at first, but, finding that the doorkeeper only grew more suspicious, ultimately agreed to being announced. The guard then told the Emperor of his doubts; upon which the latter went to a writing-table in his room, which was connected by telegraph with General Gourko's residence, and telegraphed, " Where is Gourko ? " "At home," was the reply. This of course settled the point; the false Gourko was at once arrested, and turned out to be a member of the revolutionary committee.

Filled with such thoughts, we shall not find it strange, as now we enter the imperial bed-chamber, to find that even here the horrors of

THE BREAKFAST ROOM.

his life pursued the Czar and made his nights a hideous mockery of rest. One night, not long before Alexander's assassination, one of the servants, who stood high in his master's favor, thought that he heard the Czar's voice calling him, and entered the Imperial bedroom. The Emperor, awakened suddenly by the noise of his footsteps, and not recognizing the valet in the dim light of the lamp which swung over his head, drew a revolver from beneath his pillow and fired. The servant fell to the floor with a groan. The room was quickly filled with watchmen, members of the household and courtiers, fearful that another attempt had been made on the Czar's life. When the truth was learned, the wounded man was carried to another room, and doctors pronounced his injury to be fatal. Efforts were made on all sides to prevent the news getting abroad, and it was generally given out among the people that the man had died by his own hand.

Naturally then, ere we leave the Winter Palace with all its splendor and its fearful memories, we desire to look at the sad face which has here haunted us so long. It is that of the late unhappy Czar. There are here few traces of his great beauty and magnificent physique, for the last years of his reign altered him greatly. The settled melancholy, which has always haunted the Romanoffs, apparently reached in him its climax. For his eyes, said to have been

THE CZAR'S BED-ROOM.

always sad, have here an almost pathetic expression, as though the spectres of conspiracy, assassination, Nihilism, disappointment and thwarted ambition preyed vulture-like upon his heart, and as though he half foresaw the awful doom which Destiny was holding in her hand, waiting until the fatal hour should come. That hour came all too soon, and proved more tragic even than his wildest dream could have imagined!

It was on the 21st of March, 1881, that the remains of poor Alexander were conveyed with solemn and imposing pageantry from this Winter Palace to the Cathedral on the opposite border of the river. Not a year before, the body of the Empress had also been borne over the same route to the same rest-ing-place of the Romanoffs. So long was the mournful proces-sion that it took two hours to pass a given point. It was of almost unexampled splendor, for all that was regal and warlike in the Empire had its representation there. The funeral car itself was of ebony and silver, and was drawn by eight black horses shrouded in sable draperies, while the coffin of the Czar was almost hidden by a golden pall lined with white satin. Sixteen gen-erals held the silken cords of the canopy above this, and behind his murdered father walked Alex-ander III. in his Imperial solitude, bearing alone his griefs and his responsibilities.

ALEXANDER II.

If possible, more solemn still must have been the sight of the silent thousands who lined the shores of the Neva with one vast sea of pale and saddened faces. Bareheaded and mute they stood there thus for hours ; many of them praying for the soul of the dead Czar, while hundreds of priests, clad in their ecclesiastical robes and bearing tapers in their hands, were chanting on the air a solemn requiem.

And yet, there is another side to all this story. For, however much we may pity the haunted Czar, and however friendly we may feel to the Imperial family *as individuals*, there is something which calls more loudly for our sympathy than Alexander's tragic fate, namely, the pitiable condition of the Russian people! For the last few years especially, the long bleak roads leading to Siberia have been crowded day and night with caravans of men and women of all classes of society. Not long ago there were at one time twenty thousand of these wretched victims of suspicious tyranny awaiting transportation; and during the reign of the late Alexander, at least one hundred and twenty thousand are said to have been exiled to Siberia. In these pitiable processions were not only abandoned criminals. Often the great mass of them have been *political* offenders; that is, patriotic Poles, journalists, students, poets, and even fair young women, like Vera Sassulitch, condemned at the age of sixteen to an existence worse than death.

Can there be anything worse than this? Yes, it is the fact that many of such exiles have been sentenced without a trial, and by the mere arbitrary decree of that inquisition of the nineteenth century, the Russian secret police! This is a system of espionage and absolutism worthy only of Asia. All classes of society are open to its dread inspection, and every word or look may be interpreted as treason by some lurking spy. This body has the power of seizing men and women in the dead of night and throwing them into prison, on a mere suspicion or the complaint of some enemy. And there they may be kept for months and years, and finally even exiled to Siberia without having had a public trial! In such cases inquiry after them is useless. They have been secretly arrested. They have disappeared. What becomes of them must ever be to their loved ones an agonized conjecture.

Sometimes, it is claimed, there is no shadow of reason for the arrest, save that the eye of some lecherous official has fallen upon the beauty of some beloved wife or daughter, who is thus left without a protector at the mercy of the merciless.

When, then, we shudder at the deeds of the Nihilists, let us ask ourselves what *we* would do, if we saw *our* loved ones dragged thus mysteriously to death or exile, no one knows which; and if we were liable to share the same fate, if we asked the reason why. For my part, I do not find it strange that a country thus governed should be honeycombed with revolution, and that all society should be one vast bed of dynamite ready for the first spark to blow the whole system of absolutism into the air.

Such feelings are intensified as we approach again the Neva, and view in the distance on the opposite bank the gloomy fortress of Petro-Paulovsky. This is the Bastile of Russia, the most famous,

THE FORTRESS.

or rather the most in-famous, of all its strongholds of despotism. I suppose no prison now standing in the world has witnessed so much suffering, injustice and cruelty within its walls as this. Walls, it is said, have ears; but had they tongues, what horrible deeds could be disclosed by the dark, icy dungeons of this prison below the level of the Neva, with walls and floors slimy with dampness! Such, for example, as when Alexis, the son of Peter the Great, was put to death here by his father's order; or when all the political prisoners here were drowned in their dungeons during the overflow of the Neva. Among them was the beautiful young Princess Tarakonoff, who was hated by Catharine as a possible claimant of the throne, and who had been lured back to Russia from a happy life in Italy through the brutal cunning of the Imperial favorite, Orloff.

It is said that her screams and piteous entreaties brought even her jailers to her cell; and when she bade them see how with the incoming flood from the Neva the icy water had risen already to her waist, and begged to be transferred to another cell, she received the answer, " No one leaves here without the order of the Empress." The grating was shut, and the poor young Princess was left with the rest to drown in the freezing waters of the Neva!

But from this Russian fortress, where many suspected (and God knows how many innocent) men and women are now languishing, let us cross the river by the handsome Neva bridge, while we recall one more of the many tragedies connected with that fortress-prison.

In a damp dungeon there, was once imprisoned a young man named Batenkof, suspected of conspiracy against the Czar Nicholas. How long do you imagine he remained there ? Twenty-three years ! During that time he languished in a cell below the Neva without seeing or speaking to a soul save his jailer, or rather jailers, — for he outlived three ! At the end of eleven years they allowed him the luxury of a pipe; at the end of thirteen years they gave him the Bible ; finally, after twenty-three years, they opened his prison doors. But when he was led into the court-yard, blinded by the light and oppressed by the air, he fell on his knees, weeping.

He tried to beg to be reconducted to his dungeon. I say " tried," for he could not find words to express his desire. He had forgotten how to speak. Think of the agony which a man must have suffered to reach a point like that !

Filled with these and many other gloomy memories, I suddenly found myself, appropriately enough, before the equestrian statue of the Czar Nicholas, the predecessor of the late Alexander. As I gazed upon the figure of this man, whose reign was the very personification of iron military despotism, the man who swore that he would make a Siberia of Poland and a Poland of Siberia, and up to 1848 had transported thither sixty thousand Poles, I could but ask myself, Is this Romanoff dynasty and the system it upholds worth maintaining at the price they cost? No matter how the age advances, with Nicholas, with Alexander, and with the present Czar the idea is still the same, namely, that *one man out of eighty millions has the divine authority to rule the others in the same way that his barbarous ancestors used, centuries ago!*   But the Russian people are no longer the savage hordes which once selected their most ferocious chief as sovereign. They are men born in the nineteenth century, who see that every other land in western Europe has a constitution and some representation by the people.   Here, however, there is nothing of this; no

STATUE OF THE CZAR NICHOLAS.

freedom of the press; no chance of appeal or remonstrance; while the sentiment of Trepoff, the infamous chief of police shot by Vera Sassulitch, is this: "The man who dares speak of a constitution in Russia deserves to have a bullet sent through his skull!"

Away, then, with any form of government which can only be maintained at the cost of the lives and happiness of thousands of unoffending people, who have the same right to their lives and happiness that the accident of birth gives to the Czar !

But, leaving these political reflections, let us approach a very prominent building in St. Petersburg, the Hermitage. It was built by Catharine II., just as Frederick the Great built near Berlin his palace of Sans-Souci, as a refuge from the cares of state.

Here the Empress passed many of her evenings, surrounded by French philosophers, musicians and artists ; all of whom were obliged, according to the laws of the Hermitage, to leave behind them at the threshold all considerations of rank and precedence, and to meet on terms of perfect equality.

· Before we enter the Hermitage by yonder portal supported by colossal granite giants, let me point out to you the open window in the upper story

THE HERMITAGE.

of the adjoining Winter Palace. In that room, guarded night and day, are kept most of the crown jewels of Russia. How many millions of dollars were represented in the little room where we beheld them! There I saw the Imperial Crown of the Czar, than which it would be difficult to imagine anything more magnificent. It is in the form of a dome, the summit being formed of a cross of large diamonds resting on an immense ruby. This ruby with its cross is poised upon arches of diamonds, whose bases rest upon a circle of twenty-eight other diamonds, which clasp the brow of the Emperor. The cross of the Empress also contains no less than one hundred splendid diamonds, and is perhaps the most beautiful mass of these precious stones ever formed into a single ornament.

Chief among that magnificent collection, — a detailed description of which would be impossible, — is the grand Orloff diamond, the largest in the world. An officer drew back a curtain, and revealed it to us, sparkling on the summit of the Imperial sceptre. The history of this diamond is as interesting as the stone itself is dazzling. It formed at one time the eye of an idol in a temple of India. A French soldier, pretending to have been converted to its religion, gained admission to this temple one dark night, and, by means of some surgical operation best known to himself, deprived the deity of his bright eye, and fled with the prize. After passing through several hands, it was finally purchased for over half a million of dollars by the famous Count Orloff, who laid it here in the Hermitage at the feet of Catharine II., as the most magnificent jewel in the world.

As we prepare to enter this palace, we can but remember how many of Catharine's discarded favorites have passed over these very steps, smothering under forced smiles and honeyed words their inward rage and indignation; for when Catharine wearied of her favorites she sent them an order to travel for their health, and they prudently set out at once. On arriving at the first stage of their journey, however, they were usually consoled by finding elegant presents awaiting them, — such as diamonds, money, or serfs, or frequently an estate, to which they were advised to immediately retire. If now we pass within one of the many elegant galleries of the Hermitage, we shall find that it is no longer a royal residence, but that, like the Louvre at Paris, it has now become the Imperial museum of the capital.

Here (as before, in the Library) we are amazed at the valuable art treasures which this young nation has been able to secure. The

GALLERY IN THE HERMITAGE.

truth is, for many years the Russian Government has spent large sums of money in this direction, and to-day has agents all over Europe, ready to outbid the world for any masterpiece which by chance may be offered for sale. Here is certainly the best collection of Spanish pictures to be found outside of Spain; one room alone containing no less than thirty genuine Murillos, some of which seemed to me as fine as any I had seen in Madrid and Seville. Moreover, as we walk through these galleries of beauty, we become speedily convinced that in no other art-museum in the world are there such *ornaments* as in this Hermitage. The immense vases of porphyry, stands of Siberian marble, tables of malachite, candelabra of violet jasper, and urns of lapis-lazuli, which adorn every room, are of incalculable value, and would almost in themselves repay a special visit to Russia.

The many lovely statues which this Hermitage contains are all the works of modern sculptors, but are perhaps none the less attractive on that account to the majority of travellers. As we looked upon them we were not disposed to doubt the statement that the late Alexander, who himself selected many of these statues, was a man of excellent taste and an unerring judgment in matters of art. Surely, then, a hermit might boldly forswear the rest of the world, if he could only make this Hermitage his cell; for here the marvels of the globe surround him, — glowing upon canvas, crystallized in marble, carved in ivory and woven in tapestry, presenting thus in epitome countless illustrations of the world's beauty and progress.

But now, by way of variety, let us leave the streets of St. Petersburg itself, and make an excursion to one of its charming suburbs, — to Czars-Koe-Selo, one of the summer homes of the Imperial family. It is only fifteen miles distant from the city, and can be easily reached by a railroad which was the first ever built in Russia.

Catharine II. loved this place especially, and spent enormous sums on its embellishment. Originally every statue, ornament, and pedestal of the façade of the palace, which is no less than twelve hundred feet in length, was heavily plated with gold. When, however, after a few years, the gilding wore off, and the contractors engaged to repair it offered the Empress nearly half a million of dollars for the fragments which remained, the extravagant Catharine made the scornful answer, "I am not in the habit, gentlemen, of selling my old clothes!" The avenue leading to this palace is oddly decorated with four Chinese statues, apparently smoking here in Oriental calm. One day as Catharine was taking here her usual promenade, she thought she detected on the face of one of these

CZARS-KOE-SELO.

figures a faint smile. In astonishment she observed it more closely! It surely was no fancy! The eyes actually returned her gaze with a peculiar look of admiration, which to a connoisseur like the Empress spoke volumes, and seemed remarkably human! Catharine was not a woman to be nervous or timid at anything, and accordingly she walked straight towards the statue in order to solve the mystery. She *was*, however, for a moment startled, when all these figures suddenly leaped from their pedestals, and, hats in hand, begged her to pardon the little surprise with which they had tried to enliven her Majesty's morning walk; for, in fact, her favorite Potemkin and three other courtiers had, in jest, exactly copied in dress and attitude the Chinese figures which we see.

As for the interior of the palace, there is the same lavish expenditure which characterizes the outer walls; while nothing can exceed the oddity of its furnishing. One apartment is called the Chinese room, because its furniture and decorations are modelled after some styles of the Celestial Empire. More remarkable than this is the amber room, whose walls are covered with that precious substance ; while still more famous than either is the lapis-lazuli apartment, the sides of which are beautifully inlaid with that rare stone, while the floor is of ebony, adorned with mosaic flowers made of mother-of-pearl ! Can you imagine a contrast more original and effective ? Entirely different, and in striking contrast to these splendid halls, is the small room used by the Czar as his study. It is very plainly furnished, its chief decoration consisting in the numerous portraits of his children, relatives, and soldiers which cover the walls. Whether the old domestic who conducted us through the palace suspected that we were about to drop dynamite in this room, I know not ; but he was quite reluctant to admit us into this private study of the

THE CHINESE ROOM.

Emperor. Our guide, therefore, called him aside, and whispered to him that we were really Russians of high rank who (since we were travelling incognito) were talking a foreign language. I was not

THE CZAR'S STUDY.

responsible for this awful lie; but either that or a rouble slipped into his hand produced the desired effect, and we were at once admitted. When, therefore, we came forth from the palace, a friend recalled to me the experience of two Americans who on their travels in Russia were urged by their guide to adopt Russian names. These, however, were so difficult alike to pronounce and to remember that at last they invented some for themselves suited to their professions. Thus one, who practised dentistry, called himself Count Pull-a-toothsky; while the other, who was a distiller, styled himself Prince Cask-o'-wiski!

But let us glance at a portion of the lovely park of Czars-Koe-Selo, which is no less than eighteen miles in circumference. Upon its pretty lake the young daughter of the Czar Nicholas used to feed some pet swans, of which she was very fond. This child died at an early age; and ever since then the white swans which she loved have been replaced by black ones, as though they were in mourning for their little mistress. In one of the beautiful pavilions which rise from the border of the lake hangs the portrait of this youthful princess, and beneath it is one of her childish sayings, which startles us when we think it was applied to the despotic ruler Nicholas, who must have been a very different man in his own family. It is this: "I know, papa, that you have no greater pleasure than that of making my mamma happy." Beyond the lake a pretty river winds through this park in graceful curves, repeatedly spanned

PARK OF CZARS-KOE-SELO.

by bridges, of the most fantastic and beautiful designs.   This garden
of Czars-Koe-Selo is probably the most carefully kept park in the
world ; for, on account of the severity of the Russian climate, its trees
and flowers are watched and cared for with the most anxious tender-

THE DRIVE-WAY.

ness.   Catharine II. used to say, " In Russia we have not summer
and winter, but only a white winter and a green winter."   At all
events an old invalid soldier here commands an army of five or six
hundred gardeners.   After every falling leaf a veteran runs ; and
every spear of grass is carefully drawn out of lake and river.   The
cost of all this lavish care amounts, it is said, to fifty thousand dollars
a year ; but the result is that the park is kept in the order of a ball-
room.

But, ere we take our leave of Czars-Koe-Selo, let us glance for a
moment down one of its long driveways, straight and unswerving as
an arrow.   Its monotony is relieved at intervals by lofty arches,
each one of which is surmounted by a tiny summer house, like a

jewel mounted in a ring. The sight of it reminds me of one of the mad freaks of the Czar Paul I., the half-insane son of Catharine II., whose mad whims led him now to cause ladies to descend from their carriages in the mud when he passed, and now to send an entire regiment to Siberia because it made a blunder in manœuvring. Let me cite for you one of the many stories told of his wild fancies. One day as he was returning from St. Petersburg to this palace, he saw a soldier whose face pleased him. He stopped his carriage, and beckoned the man to approach. He did so, trembling from head to

foot. "What are you, Dust of the earth?" asked the Czar. (This was Paul's pleasant way of addressing his subjects!) The dust of the earth replied, "A private in your Majesty's regiment." "You lie," replied Paul; "you are a lieutenant." And he ordered him to get up beside the coachman. At the end of the next quarter of a mile the Czar touched him with his sword. "What are you?" he again demanded. "A

PETERHOF.

lieutenant, Sire, thanks to your Majesty's kindness." "You lie," replied Paul; "you are a captain." At the end of another quarter the Emperor struck him again. "What are you, Dust of the earth?" "A captain, your Majesty." "You lie," Paul cried again; "you are a major." By the time they reached the palace the lucky soldier was a general. If the distance had been a little greater, he might have become commander-in-chief!

Still more attractive than Czars-Koe-Selo is Peterhof, another summer residence of the Imperial family, which we may visit before returning to St. Petersburg. It is connected with the capital not only by rail, but by a line of admirable steamboats, which every hour ply back and forth along the river Neva and the Gulf of Finland, beside the gigantic fortresses of Cronstadt.

No sooner do we enter the great park of Peterhof than we find ourselves surrounded by a multitude of fountains, which in number, design and beauty are unsurpassed, even by those of Versailles. This also is a result of the indomitable energy and ambition of Peter the Great. Louis XIV. had created fountains on the sandy plain of Versailles. Why should not he do as much along the marshes of the Neva? Within two months after the autocrat's order had been given, the thousands of workmen who had been summoned to the prodigious task announced that the canals and aqueducts were ready. Other laborers were equally expeditious in the construction of palaces, avenues, and villas. Statues and ornaments sprang up as if by magic; and, since trees were already abundant, the entire park and buildings were constructed within a single year! In his impatience, Peter is said to have felled many trees himself, swinging the axe with a force which none of his workmen could rival.

The fountains, however, form the most remarkable feature of the place. There seems no limit to their number and variety. One is called the "Mountain of Gold," because the water flows over a flight of gilded steps, thus giving it (especially when the fountains are illuminated) the appearance of a cataract of molten gold. Nymphs, lions, river-gods, the heroes of mythology and history, all figure in these fountains, until the combination is bewildering; while, not content with these, the architect has designed long rows of single fountains, without statues, and *pyramids of water* formed by five hundred and twenty-five jets, and *artificial trees,* each leaf of which sends forth a silvery stream of water ; the whole producing a beautiful effect. Most astonishing of all, however, is the "Cascade of Samson" under the palace windows. Here Samson is contending with a lion, from whose mouth leaps forth a flood of water to a height of eighty feet! Finally, the enormous flood of water from these fountains is gathered in one mighty channel, and rolls away like some wild mountain torrent toward the sea.

It is said to have been one of the fancies of the Czar Nicholas to make his pages and servants charge upon a number of these fountains at the beat of the drum, and, rushing furiously into the blinding streams, to capture them like batteries, and turn the water off with their own hands. We may be tolerably sure, however, that Nicholas never tried it himself! A much more agreeable story of his life here is that connected with a little island on one of the pretty lakes which he caused to be formed out of the marshes that till his time had adjoined the grounds at Peterhof. Upon this island is an Italian villa, precisely like one near Palermo, Sicily, where the Emperor and Empress passed the winter of 1846. Nicholas, perceiving how charmed the Empress was with that Italian residence, gave secret orders to have its counterpart erected here at Peterhof ; which, to her great surprise and delight, she found awaiting her, filled with rare works of art and souvenirs of their Italian winter.

In one of the ponds of Peterhof are tame fishes, as old, it is said as the time of Catharine Second. A white-haired pensioned soldier has no other duty than that of calling these fishes to the surface by the ringing of a bell. The fish, however, do not display themselves for nothing any more than does the pensioned soldier ; for, while he expects a rouble, they anticipate and receive some crumbs of cake which they devour eagerly. We could hardly feel flattered, therefore, by the reception given us by these fishes of Peterhof ; for no sooner were the crumbs exhausted than they turned their backs upon us, and sought again the privacy of their own apartments.

A visit to Peterhof reminds us of an incident told of Prince

Bismarck when he was the Prussian ambassador at the Czar's court,
and which admirably illustrates Russian absolutism. He was standing one day at a window of the palace with Alexander II., when
he observed a sentinel in the centre of a spacious lawn, with

THE BALL-ROOM AT PETERHOF.

apparently nothing whatever to guard. Out of curiosity he inquired
of the Emperor why the man was stationed there. Alexander turned
to an aide-de-camp. "Count Schoufalof, why is that soldier stationed
there ? "   " I do not know, your Imperial Majesty."   The Czar
frowned, and answered curtly, " Send me the officer in command
for the day."   Presently the officer appeared, pale with apprehension. " Prince Ivanovitch Poniatowsky, why is a sentinel stationed

on that lawn?" "Really, your Majesty, I—I do not know," stammered the officer. "Not know?" cried the Czar in surprise; "request then the general in command of the troops at Peterhof to present himself immediately." A few moments later the commandant hurried to the spot in a state of great fear and agitation. "General Petrovitch Tschernischewski Bogoljubof Nijninovgorodinski," asked the Czar, "will you be kind enough to inform us why that soldier is stationed in yonder isolated place?" "I beg to inform your Majesty that it is in accordance with an ancient custom," replied the general, evasively. "What was the origin of the custom?" inquired Bismarck. "I—I do not at present recollect," stammered the officer. "Investigate the subject, and report the result," the Czar said. Accordingly the investigation began, and after three days and nights of labor, it was ascertained that, about *eighty years before*, one morning in spring, Catharine II.

STATUE OF PETER THE GREAT.

observed in the centre of this lawn the first Mayflower of the season lifting its delicate head above the lately frozen soil. She ordered a soldier to stand there to prevent its being plucked. The order was duly inscribed upon the books; and thus for eighty years, summer and winter, a sentinel had stood upon that spot, no one apparently, until Prince Bismarck's time, caring to question the reason of the custom!

But, taking our leave of Peterhof, we soon arrive again within the limits of St. Petersburg, where, having thus made the circuit of the city, we stand with admiration and respect before the colossal statue of that extraordinary man, who conceived and executed the daring plan of building here the great metropolis, on which he seems to gaze with pride. He is represented as reining in his steed at full gallop on the very verge of a precipice, his face turned toward the Neva, and his outstretched hand apparently calling on the world to witness the triumphant result of his indomitable will. Even the huge block of granite which forms the pedestal is itself remarkable; for it is one enormous mass weighing fifteen hundred tons, brought hither from Finland with immense labor. It was on this very mass of rock that Peter the Great once stood and watched the victory of his infant navy over his enemies, the Swedes. Truly a wonderful man must this bold horseman have been!—so gigantic in form that we feel like pygmies beside the rod which indicates his height; so powerful that his walking-stick, still preserved in the Museum, was a bar of iron; so skilful that he made with his own hands his house, furniture and boats; so brave that he laughed to scorn his superstitious nobles, and went incognito to England, France and Holland, and studied their institutions in the humble garb of a day laborer. It is impossible to take a step in St. Petersburg without being reminded of him. Do we tread upon pavements? It is his work that we do not sink in a swamp. Do we admire its gigantic temples? It was at his command that they were reared, upon a soil into which whole forests had to be thrown; so that the foundations of St. Petersburg sink as far beneath the soil as its gilded spires rise toward heaven. And all this was done not only before the age of steam and machinery, but when his workmen carried the earth for the city ramparts in their caps and aprons!

With all his barbarity, therefore, this Peter must be called one of the world's great men. His work has survived him; and the Russian Empire, rude and almost formless in his hands, covers to-day an enormous portion of the globe, and glorifies its founder in many different languages; for from the Polar Sea to the Caspian, from Fin-

land to the Chinese wall, the name of Peter is spoken almost as of some deity. In this connection, let me lead you to the rear of this statue, and point out to you that building which of all others in St. Petersburg seems the peculiar emblem of his genius. It is the Admiralty, — the centre of the great naval department of Russia. As we behold this gigantic building, the façade of which is one-half mile in length, and remember what it represents, we can hardly wonder that the reign of Peter

THE ADMIRALTY.

the Great is considered by the Russians as well-nigh the commencement of their civilization. For think of merely this one thing which he performed. He found Russia without even a fishing-boat. He bequeathed to her a victorious navy, and established commercial relations with almost every other nation on the globe; and this, although the harbor of his capital is for six months in the year as inaccessible to ships as the North Pole itself! From the summit of this tower, which is itself adorned with columns and colossal statues, rises a slender gilded shaft, beautiful and suggestive at any time, but particularly so when on it falls the combined effulgence of the moon and northern sun ; for then this gilded lance seems like a glittering exclamation point of wonder at the vast city which floats beneath it, and which, obedient to a will that knew no obstacle, has risen to and rests upon the surface of the Neva like a fair lily with resplendent colors.   At such a time the faults of this great city of the North, due largely to its youth and rapid growth, all disappear beside the marvellous fact that it exists at all.   Having then since the era of its founder made such gigantic strides of progress, we can but hope that this city of Peter the Great will achieve still more brilliant triumphs in that glorious future which *emancipated, educated,* and *constitutionalized* Russia will one day inevitably enjoy.

MOSCOW

THE CITIES OF THE CZAR.

II.

MOSCOW.

IF you care to glance at a map of Russia, you will see that Moscow is situated four hundred and three miles southeast of St.
Petersburg, and the railroad which connects them is a line of unde-
viating straightness. When the engineers who were to construct it
had so designed the route that by occasional turnings it might pass
through several prominent towns, they submitted their plan to the
Czar Nicholas for approval.

"Bring me a map!" exclaimed the autocrat, pushing aside the
papers. The map was procured.

"Where is Moscow?"

"There, your Majesty."

"And where is St. Petersburg?"

"There, your Majesty."

"Then," exclaimed the Czar, imperiously, drawing a straight line
between the cities, "make the railroad there!"

Accordingly the road was constructed straight and unswerving as
an arrow, with a total disregard of the towns in its vicinity. It
leaves them contemptuously in the distance, and they must be
reached from the station in droschkies or sleighs, according to the
season. It would be wearisome to describe this long and monotonous
journey. Hour after hour passes, yet we can perceive almost no
change in the surrounding scenery. An endless ocean of pine and
fir trees tosses its green waves afar off to an almost limitless horizon,

11

MOSCOW.

and dreary uncultivated wastes impress us with a melancholy sense
of the vastness of this northern realm. This feeling is intensified
when at one place we cross the river Volga, the history of whose
shores has been so dark and savage that we should hardly be surprised to see its waters tinged with blood. From this point down-
wards the Volga is navigable for steamers, and we might step on

board of one and sail through a little strip of Russian territory two thousand miles and more in length, as far as Astrachan, on the Caspian Sea! At last, however, about eighteen hours from St. Petersburg, we gain our first view of Moscow, and realize with delight that before us is the Mecca of our Russian pilgrimage; the old Muscovite capital, the picture of whose battlements and towers has haunted us from childhood. I do not wonder that the soldiers of Napoleon's army, after their weary march of thousands of miles, shouted with a frenzy of enthusiasm as this beautiful panorama of Moscow burst upon their view. In fact, no traveller can gaze upon it without deep emotion; for, like Constantinople, it is a border city, standing on the confines of the Eastern and Western worlds. We have now reached a place whose longitude is further east than that of Jerusalem, and where the two great divisions of our globe, the Orient and Occident, gaze into each other's eyes. Beyond this glittering city are vast uncultivated regions, spreading out in barbaric wildness as far as the great kingdoms of Tartary and China, or over the frozen plains of Siberia to the broad Pacific; and almost reaching Alaska, our own frost-covered storm-door of the North. But as a great continent rises slowly from the sea, so out of the wide-spread barbarism of these eastern lands the huge empire of Russia is emerging, and Moscow is its lofty headland, its frontier city, faced Janus-like, to the East and West, a connecting link between the Russia which has been and that which is to be.

But in the midst of these reflections our train has crossed the river Moskwa — which has given its name to the city — and has entered the railroad station. It is an edifice whose modern air makes us at first doubt our arrival in this ancient capital of the Czar. Yet the mere fact that a railroad (the great modern agent of civilization) has here a terminus, is no proof that the city is in all respects similarly advanced. It was at this station that I bade adieu to some Russian acquaintances, one of whom (a French lady who had married a Muscovite) assured me that there were still in good Russian society traces of the old custom of tying up wives by their hair and flogging them.

At least, many husbands when angry struck their wives as a matter of course, and not unfrequently even used a whip on their fair shoulders. "Incredible!" you say. So I thought and said, at first; but that such barbarities are not unknown in Russia I was convinced by a score of stories which she narrated to me in proof of the fact.

Fatigued by the long night-journey from St. Petersburg, we entered the ancient city of the Czars in one of those abominable Russian droschkies, whose motion is something like riding on the back of a runaway camel. Before us extended one of the characteristic streets of Moscow, with its confused mingling of churches, palaces and hovels, and with a pavement of muddy earth, into which sharp stones have been occasionally dumped, like raisins in a pudding. As for the lighting of these streets, not long ago a Muscovite coun-

CONTRASTS IN ARCHITECTURE.

cillor argued that people who go out at night should carry their own lamps! Fortunately, however, his decision was overruled, and at present the avenues of Moscow are supplied with gaslights.

Five minutes after we had left the railway station, we needed no argument to convince us of the truth of the statement that Moscow is one of the most irregularly built cities in the world. In truth, it is precisely characteristic of a nation in a transition state.

Every building seems strangely placed in striking contrast to its neighbor. Here, for instance, is a finely proportioned church with lofty towers and brilliant cupola; but before it is the simple hut of a blacksmith, and on one side extends a row of common yellow cottages. For in Moscow miserable hovels, which we should expect to find only in the outskirts of a town, stand forth unblushingly beside a palace or cathedral; just as one of those Russian peasants, whose acquaintance we made in St. Petersburg, when clad in his sheepskin coat, wherein are concentrated the vile smells of several generations, will stand quite unconscious of his filthiness, beside a man who is cleanly dressed. The more cultured Russians are themselves keenly alive to this, but so far from being ashamed of acknowledging it, they do so with a laugh. When I one day frankly stated to two of them my surprise at the savage appearance of the natives, and the odd blending of edifices in Moscow, they laughed at my modest way of criticism, and said twice as much against these features as I had done. One of them, who had spent most of his time in France, pointed to the streets of Moscow with disdain, adding with a sneer, " Ça ne me plaît pas du tout;" while the other shrugged his shoulders and said with a laugh, "Give us time; Rome was not built in a day."

One of the first things to attract our attention in riding through this city was the enormous number of churches it contains. Their architecture is peculiar. How singular, for instance, is the style of their cupolas. To use a homely but correct comparison, their form resembles closely that of an inverted onion; but it is far from being displeasing to the eye, when one is accustomed to its strangeness. On the contrary, as these bulbous domes are usually gilded, and gleam resplendent in the sun, they are among the most attractive and brilliant architectural ornaments in the world. Moreover, one fact in relation to these churches we hail with genuine satisfaction, — namely, that beneath those glittering domes no distinctions are ever made between rich and poor. Upon their marble pavement are no favored places, obtainable by money or by birth. There at least, even in Russia, noble and serf meet upon terms of absolute equality, and side by side they offer up their prayers to God.

Occasionally we passed the house of some wealthy Russian nobleman, whose name we usually found impossible either to pronounce or remember, but for whom we at least had time to feel profound commiseration. For how wearisome and exasperating the residents of St. Petersburg and Moscow must have found the police regulations maintained there for the past few years! At the door of each of these houses is stationed a *dvornik*, or porter, who is at the same time a servant of the proprietor and an agent of the police. Thus he not only has to sweep the steps and build the fires, but he must also guard against suspicious characters, and even see that the inmates conduct themselves like loyal subjects and faithfully observe all passport regulations.

Formerly, it is said, these watchmen used to aid the police in robbing and waylaying citizens. At all events, there is little doubt that between thieves and policemen a resident of Moscow leads a troubled life. Nowhere is the system of corruption (so frightfully prevalent in Russia) more incorrigible than in the police force. It has not been an uncommon thing for the wealthy citizens of Moscow and St. Petersburg to pay to the police a kind of thief-insurance money ; and strange to say, whenever the payments were regular, their property was unmolested. There is a story that some time ago a Moscow jailer was discovered to be in the habit of letting out a notorious burglar every night, on condition that he should return before morning and share with him the booty. When at last the burglar was caught, the secret came to light. The turnkey confessed his fault, but threw all the blame upon the chief jailer, who, he said, received the lion's share of the spoils. The chief jailer also confessed his sin, but pleaded that the police took from him almost everything which he had thus gained. Finally the affair became so complicated that the following laughable result was reached. The burglar was tried, but through some technicality was acquitted, the turnkey was not even indicted, while the jailer was simply transferred to another prison.

There is one building of ominous interest in Moscow, whose towers seem to have the cruel sharpness of a pair of tusks. It is the Moscow Tribunal. When a man is brought here for a real or supposed political offence, there are two modes of dealing with him.

He may be tried before a regular tribunal, or put, as it is called, "under inspection." In the former case, if convicted, he will be condemned to prison or be transported to Siberia. If put "under inspection," he is removed without any trial to some distant part of Russia, where he is compelled to live under the strict surveillance of the police. This is the usual mode of dealing with a person supposed to be dangerous, although no sufficient proof of treason can be found to actually condemn him. After spending four, six, and perhaps ten years under police supervision near the White Sea or the Ural Mountains, the suspected man, if he has behaved quietly, is usually

"THE TRIBUNAL."

informed, without any explanation, that he may go to live anywhere except in St. Petersburg and Moscow! Is it strange that there is discontent in a country like this?

As for the chance of obtaining justice, even when a trial is permitted, sad stories are told of Russian judges, which do not tend to increase one's confidence in them. It is commonly said that a Russian judge can always be bribed to acquit, unless the other side has already induced him to convict; and even then he can be prevailed upon to pass a mild sentence, unless the other side has already hired him to pronounce a severe one. However this may be, one of the most amazing things which I heard in Russia was the remark of a nobleman, with whom I travelled from St. Petersburg to Moscow. I had asked him, "To which side do the sympathies of the judges naturally incline when you noblemen have a lawsuit with the peasantry?" His reply was so extraordinary that I desire to give it in his exact words. It was this, "Quand on a de l'argent, il est facile de faire tout ce que l'on veut avec les juges" (When one has money it is easy to do anything one wishes with the judges). This was told me by a Russian nobleman, whose brother was in the private suite of the Czar.

Not far from my hotel in Moscow was a fantastically colored structure, known as the "Red Gate." In point of beauty it would be a blessing to the city if either the Nihilists or the thunderbolts of heaven were to destroy it at once. And yet it was erected one hundred and thirty years ago by the merchants of Moscow, in honor of the coronation of the daughter of Peter the Great. Surely here was an occasion for a nobler arch than this. For the green and red colors of its stucco covering are faded like a calico curtain; its cheap statues look like mammoth Punch and Judy figures; and its plaster coating has been broken off in so many places that the whole portal looks as if pitted with the small-pox.

THE RED GATE.

But scarcely have we left this gateway before we discern in the distance another arch of triumph which at first commands our admiration. For although we have not quite forgotten the stucco of St. Petersburg, yet we cannot believe that an arch of these proportions, which bears the proud name of Alexander I., and which was erected to commemorate the expulsion of the

French from Russia, can be anything but genuine. But, alas! on close examination we find that this also is covered with the detestable Russian plaster, which is now peeling off in sections; while the horses, the car itself, and the statue of Victory above are all of cast-iron, not of bronze! This is the more sad when we remember, — what we discovered in St. Petersburg and shall also see exemplified in Moscow, — that when Russia really puts forth the effort, she can and does surpass the modern world in the solidity and splendor of her temples and columns; for the treasures of her quarries are exhaustless and the skill of her lapidaries unexcelled.

THE ARCH OF VICTORY.

Of this I was never more thoroughly convinced than when, after passing these unworthy arches, I approached the famous "Church of the Saviour," an edifice the splendor of which is destined to outshine that of almost any other temple in the world. It was commenced in 1813, and was designed to commemorate the defeat of the French. It is a most imposing structure, visible from every quarter of the city, and combining majesty of proportion with elegance of decoration. The stone is of a delicate cream color, the beauty of which is enhanced by the azure of the Russian sky against which it stands relieved. It is of course in the form of the Greek cross, and all its domes gleam like the sun in gilded splendor; while around the walls extends a long frieze of life-size figures. Yet, beautiful as it thus appears, its exterior is only a faint hint of the treasures which its walls enclose. These of themselves would repay a special journey to Russia. The floor is of checkered marble, and the walls are covered with beautiful expanses of Siberian jasper, porphyry, malachite and alabaster, all

THE CHURCH OF THE SAVIOUR.

polished to the highest degree, cut in a great variety of forms, and gleaming like the surface of a mirror. Here and there these splendid ornaments are interspersed with life-size or colossal mosaic portraits or pictures, frequently incrusted with jewels, — while the mighty dome itself is filled with a wonderful and awe-inspiring painting of the Trinity. I saw this cathedral under the disadvantage of its being partially filled with scaffoldings and workmen; but I came forth from it convinced that, when completed, this will be the second, if not the first, cathedral in the world, for splendor. I do not dare to hazard an estimate of its entire cost, and I have found none that I can accept with confidence. Let me only remark, as an example, that one comparatively small section of Siberian jasper, inserted like a medallion in a marble wall, cost no less than $15,000.

Moreover, it should be remembered that this is the second great cathedral which Russia has built during the last seventy years; the famous one of St. Isaac's, in St. Petersburg, having been begun in 1819, and completed in 1858, after an expenditure of about twenty million dollars. A third cathedral, nearly as large, is also in process of construction at Nijni Novgorod. Marvellously beautiful is this Church of the Saviour, in the long fascinating Northern twilight which makes the Russian summer so attractive.

> "Oh the splendor of the city
>   When the sun is in the west !
> Ruddy gold on spire and belfry,
>   Gold on Moskwa's placid breast ;
> Till the twilight, soft and sombre,
>   Falls on wall and street and square,
> And the domes and towers in shadow
>   Stand like silent monks at prayer."

Russia is, outwardly at least, one of the most religious countries on the globe. In my walks through Moscow I repeatedly passed a gate, where at almost every hour of the day is gathered a crowd of kneeling worshippers. For here is a miraculous picture, called the Iberian Mother of God. It seems hardly credible, but I have it on the best authority, that the priests of this chapel receive in donations no less than fifty thousand dollars a year ! Every Orthodox Russian, as he passes this chapel, takes off his hat and crosses himself; and even the Czar himself, whenever he visits Moscow, always dismounts and prays before this image of the Virgin. When Napoleon, in 1812, was advancing upon Moscow, the populace clamorously called upon their bishops to take the Madonna, and under her protection lead them out armed with hatchets against the hosts of the infidel.

One morning, as I was standing on the steps of the Church of the Assumption, I noticed coming rapidly along the street a handsome coach drawn by four horses. The coachman's head was bare, and all the people in the streets took off their hats and crossed themselves as it passed. Much to my astonishment, I was told that this was the carriage of the Iberian Madonna. Fortunately for me, it stopped before a neighboring house, and two priests took from the carriage the sacred painting of the Madonna, and bore it reverently into the dwelling. Two female servants on the doorsteps kneeled as they passed, so that the sacred image might be carried over their heads. Like the Holy Bambino at Rome, it was being taken to heal the sick. I did not wait until it was brought forth again, but asked my guide a question that perplexed me. If this same image could thus be taken around the city on professional visits, how was it that the persons who meantime assembled to pray at the chapel did not get impatient at its absence? "That is very simple," replied the guide; "there is a copy of this picture which takes its place in the chapel when the real one is called away, and thus neither the devotions nor the donations of the faithful suffer interruption; for no worshipper can tell the difference between the genuine and the copy." How simple seem the tricks of trade after they are explained !

As might be expected, the theological knowledge of the Russian peasant is exceedingly limited, notwithstanding his implicit faith in religious rites and sacred pictures. An oft repeated story illustrates this. It is said that a Moujik was once asked by a priest if he could name the three persons in the Trinity. "Certainly," was the answer; "every one knows that. They are the Saviour, the Mother of God, and St. Nicholas, the miracle-worker !" Yet this is not so bad as the reply of the English university student, cited by George Eliot, who, when requested to state what he knew about Moses, answered, "Moses said to the whale, when it had cast him forth upon the land, 'Almost thou persuadest me to be a Christian'"!

One of the most picturesque and Oriental of all the shrines of Moscow is the Church of the Nativity, whose bulbous domes and pretty belfries rise as usual from an environment of low-roofed shops and dwellings. In this church especially, as well as in many others of Moscow, there occurs on Easter morning a ceremony which I regretted being too late in the season to witness. The assembled worshippers have then the privilege of saluting each other with a kiss, and of course all the "old bachelors" go to church that day, if never at any other time. The theory is, that all the Christians ought to embrace each other, to show that they are brethren in Christ. When two friends, for example, meet during that night or on Easter morning, one says, "Christ

THE CHURCH OF THE NATIVITY.

hath arisen;" the other replies, "In truth He hath arisen;" and then, in a paroxysm of joy over the good news, they kiss each other three times on the right and left cheek alternately. Moreover, this outburst of affection is frequently followed by the remark, "Come, brother, let us drink together!" and to the public house they go, where brandy flows as freely as the water of the liberated Neva.

Curious stories are told of this Russian custom. On coming out of his cabinet one Easter morning, the Czar Nicholas spoke to the guard at his door the ordinary words of salutation, "Christ hath arisen." Instead, however, of the usual reply, the Czar received the flat contradiction, "No, he has not, your Imperial

Majesty." Astounded by such an unexpected answer (for no one
ever ventured to dissent from the Czar, even in the most respect-
ful terms), he instantly demanded an explanation. The soldier
then admitted that he was a Jew, and could not conscientiously
acknowledge the fact of the resurrection. This boldness for conscience' sake so pleased the Czar that he gave the man a handsome Easter present.

In some respects Moscow is not an ideal city for the traveller.
With all its picturesque, historical and interesting objects, in point
of cleanliness it is still open to improvement. But cleanliness is to
the tourist of more practical importance even than godliness, and I
regret to say that I obtained that blessing less easily in Russia than
in Turkey, Asia Minor, Greece, Syria, Spain, or any other land which
it was ever my fortune to visit.

The "Slavianski Bazar" is the name of that hotel in Moscow
which Murray recommends as the best. I freely admit that it possesses some qualities which entitle it to praise, and it probably is the
best hotel in the city. But the fact remains that what is good for
Russia may be abominable for other parts of the world. Neatness is
still rare in Russian hotels, even in St. Petersburg and Moscow;
while the filth and discomfort of hotels in smaller towns are indescribable.

We had fine rooms in the "Slavianski," so far as furniture was
concerned, and after a fatiguing day of sight-seeing, we commended
ourselves to the care of the Iberian Madonna and lay down (as we
fondly hoped) to rest.

It was midnight, and "deep sleep had fallen upon the earth."
The sun had as usual stepped for a few moments only behind the
curtains of the night, but was already peeping forth, impatient of
even an hour's retirement. In appearance, the lodgers in the Slavianski Bazar were all peacefully sleeping. But what is this? There
are sounds of hurrying feet, shrill exclamations of disgust, and words
which would befit an argument upon eternal punishment. The light
of candles breaks upon the gloom, and lo! upon the snowy coverings
of the beds, and on the walls, the curtains and the *robes-de-nuit*

are seen a swarming host of — but no, I will not mention them. From another such sight may I be ever spared! In fact, the rooms were full of that particular kind of vermin the end and aim of whose existence seems to be to dispute with man the possession of a comfortable bed. So well had these creatures obeyed the divine injunction, "Be ye fruitful and multiply," that they were found next morning playing hide and seek upon our coats and shawls. Three also were discovered by chance luxuriating in a tooth mug, and seven unburied ones lay in the soap dish, sleeping the sleep that knows no waking!

Next morning, I conversed with the proprietor on the subject of Russian hunting by candle-light, animated by that warmth of feeling naturally inspired by a night spent either in the chase or hanging over the back of a chair. From him I gained the following information, which further experience abundantly confirmed.

"My dear sir," said the innkeeper, "it is a sad fact that in all Russian hotels you will have abundant occupation in the art of self-defence. In winter it is worse than in summer. The Russians who come here (you see I am French) from the extreme east, south and north, are not over cleanly. Many of them do not remove their clothes when they go to bed. Most of them play the part of pasture-grounds to many parasites, and thus the mattresses, the walls, the paper, and the canopies become veritable zoölogical hanging-gardens." Anxious to know the truth from the proprietor's own lips, I asked him, "Are these insects which you allude to fleas, or are they — but no, I will not mention them." "Sir," replied the Frenchman with a shrug of his shoulders, "they are both; and in winter there is added still another kind;" and bending toward my ear, he whispered a word whose English name rhymes perfectly with — *mice!* Since then I have never been able to think of some Russian hotels without feeling inclined to dance the Highland Fling.

In walking through the Muscovite capital, one frequently finds himself beside the river Moskwa, which gives its name to the city through which it flows. Were we able to raise ourselves some hundreds of feet above this river, we should see that the city lies in the form of two circles, one within the other. Both are surrounded by walls of fortification, and both represent successive periods of Moscow's growth. Through the outer circle we have already ridden.

THE KREMLIN.

But now we are to approach the inner core of the Czar's capital, the very heart of this strange city, the far-famed *Kremlin of Moscow.* Originally, this Kremlin, like the Acropolis of Athens, was surrounded by stout walls of oak, and in the centre of this strong enclosure lived the Czar, surrounded by his relatives and nobles. More than five hundred years ago, however, the wooden walls gave place to stone ones, in order that the Tartars might be more successfully resisted. Again and again, under successive shocks of war, have these old ramparts been injured and rebuilt; but in form they have always remained substantially the same, down to the present time. Within are the lofty spires and gilded domes of the most sacred temples of Russia, and the Imperial Palace of the Czars. The effect of all this is wonderfully enhanced by the vivid colors of roofs, cupolas, walls and spires, which form, in a glittering expanse of red, white, green, gold and silver, a veritable constellation of splendor! Fortunately, much of the Kremlin was unharmed by the conflagration of 1812; for the devouring element did little save to lick these battlements with its tongues of flame. I had always imagined this great Muscovite citadel blackened by time, or at least clothed in those sombre tints which seem the fitting garb of venerable monuments. Here, however, I was pleasantly disappointed. The Russians, like the

people of almost every new nation, love what is modern or appears so, and therefore they renew the colors of the Kremlin as often as they fade under the keen breath of the frosty North. Let us pass rapidly beneath the Kremlin's deeply tinted battlements, towards a lofty tower through which we shall make our entry thither. We first find ourselves in an open square outside the walls, where a group of bronze statuary attracts our notice. It represents a peasant appealing to a

THE APPROACH TO THE KREMLIN.

Russian general to save the beloved Kremlin, and to lead the armies of Russia against the advancing hosts of France. It is a strikingly suggestive group, for the peasant points eagerly upward to the towers of the Kremlin but a few paces distant.

Beyond these figures on the right, we see rising to a lofty height

the tower of the "Redeemer Gate," the most sacred of the five portals which pierce the Kremlin walls. Over this gateway is a picture of Christ, which is deemed so sacred that no one is allowed to pass beneath it without removing his hat. Even the Emperor himself does not fail to conform to this custom, whenever he rides into his Kremlin palace. I have frequently stood here half an hour at a time, watching the motley throng of passing Russians; but whether the travellers were on foot, in droschkies, or on horseback, they never failed

to uncover their heads as they crossed its threshold.

Whenever we ourselves passed through this portal, our guide would always turn around to us and give us the solemn warning,

THE CONVENT OF THE ASCENSION.

"Hats off, Gentlemen!" Formerly indeed, an omission to take off the hat here was severely punished; and even now it would not be at all advisable to refuse to comply with the custom. The true traveller, however, is always cosmopolitan enough to obligingly remove his shoes at the door of a Turkish mosque, or his hat at a " Redeemer Gate."

This gate is, however, a deep one, owing to the thickness of its tower, and hence it is with the assurance of an acquired cold in the head that we put on our hats again on the other side. We are now fairly within the Kremlin enclosure and look eagerly about us at its numerous buildings. Here, close by the sacred gate, is the Convent of the Ascension, the walls of which are tinted blue, while the dome has the color of silver. This has been a favorite place of resort for princesses or the daughters of Russian nobles, who have wished to retire from the excitements of the world to the tranquil life of the cloister. In its crypt are the tombs of many Russian empresses, one of them being that of the first wife of Peter the Great, who died there in solitude, after having been forced to take the veil. Some years before, Peter had suspected her of conspiring against him, and accordingly gave her the awful punishment of the *knout*, and banished her to this cloister forever. Hundreds of her suspected associate-conspirators were put to death, Peter himself occasionally taking a hand in their execution. One day, indeed, with a wine-glass in one hand and an axe in the other, he is said to have cut off twenty heads within an hour,—one every three minutes, and after a bumper of wine.

In one prominent building in the Kremlin enclosure were shown to us some silver kettles and golden vases, which are of the utmost sanctity,—for they contain the holy oil with which all children in Russia must be baptized, or be damned. The priests of the Greek church occupy four weeks of the year in manufacturing this oil, and then send it all over the empire to the different churches. The soul of this mixture is a homœopathic dose (of, I should think, the two-millionth potency) extracted from the oil-flask said to have been used by Mary Magdalene, when she washed the feet of Jesus. I tried to find out how Russia obtained this oil-flask of Mary, but was unsuccessful. It was a prominent bishop of Moscow who in priestly robes displayed to us these oil-jars; and so sacred a person is this priest, that it is customary for every one at parting to reverently kiss his hand. I had fully made up my mind to do this, but I confess, when I saw what kind of a hand he had, — I passed! A French gentleman, however, who was my travelling companion in Russia, slipped into this palm of doubtful complexion a rouble, which is equal to about eighty cents. I was shocked. I could not believe that so high an ecclesiastic would receive so small a fee. But, on the contrary, his fingers clutched it with the grip of Judas,

THE ST. NICHOLAS GATE.

and his face relaxed into an oleaginous smile which could not have been surpassed if his features had been dipped within the sacred kettle.

But leaving now this sacred oil-factory, a few steps further bring us to another of the Kremlin gates. If we could only push aside this sentry-box, we should see that over the entrance is suspended a miraculous picture of St. Nicholas, which is called the dread of perjurers, and the comfort of suffering humanity. For in former times it was the custom for parties in a lawsuit to take their oaths before this venerated picture, and if any one swore falsely under such circumstances, he was immediately struck dumb with lockjaw. What a pity that this image has now lost its efficacy! Otherwise we might occasionally borrow it of the Russian Government! Think how useful it would have been in the trial of our Star Route officials!

Let me tell you one other circumstance in connection with this gateway. By the order of Napoleon, the French, in abandoning Moscow, sought to blow it up. A miracle is reported to have then occurred. When the gunpowder exploded, it caused in the tower only a slight crack, which extended just as far as the frame of this image. There, however, it suddenly stopped; leaving the image, its glass covering, and even the lamp burning before it, all uninjured! The Czar Alexander caused an inscription to be placed over the

THE IVAN TOWER AND CATHEDRAL.

gate to commemorate the miracle, and those who do not believe it may go to Siberia.

But advancing now beyond the Nicholas gate, we see before us one of the most prominent of all the Kremlin structures, — the Ivan tower. This is indeed an imposing and beautiful monument, for its octagonal walls are of snowy whiteness, and at a height of three hundred and twenty-five feet, it wears a crown of gold. Built in the year 1600, this is the campanile, or bell-tower, of the Kremlin. It contains, in fact, no less than thirty-six bells, two of which are of silver, while the largest weighs one hundred and thirty thousand pounds. The mellow, sweet vibrations of a musical bell are perhaps

among the most agreeable sounds whose waves can fall upon the
human ear.   There are those who prefer them to all other kinds of
music.   Such persons should come to Russia to be satisfied; for in
Russia bells are regarded as a sacred instrument of worship, and so
much silver and gold are cast in their molten mass, that when complete, they send forth most perfect tones, which rise and fall with
a majestic harmony like the waves of the sea, or ripple out in soft
and tremulous golden and silvery notes like the tones of a bird.

But if the bells within this tower amaze us, what shall we say
when we approach its base, and survey the monster mass of metal
which rests upon the ground?   This is justly called the "King of
Bells," and looks, as we approach it, like a huge bronze tent, for
through the aperture in its side a person could enter without lower-
ing his head.   Not much idea is ever given by statistics, but let me

THE "KING OF BELLS."

remind you that the thickness of the metal is two feet, and its weight
four hundred and forty-four thousand pounds!   Moreover, within
this bell forty persons can assemble at one time, and the cavity has

been used as a chapel. Owing to an imperfection in the casting (caused, it is said, by jewels and other treasures having been thrown into the liquid metal by the ladies of Moscow), a piece, which of itself weighs eleven tons, was broken out of the side, and thus the bell was ruined. Through all the joys and sorrows in the city's history, this "King of Bells" has therefore remained silent since its birth.

But leaving the huge bell of Moscow, let us stand now before the most sacred edifice of the Kremlin, and indeed of all Russia, — the Cathedral of the Assumption. It is severely plain in its appearance, and its whitewashed walls give no hint of the treasures within, although its domes gleam as usual like golden helmets. It is within this cathedral that amid the most imposing ceremonies all the Czars from Ivan the Terrible down to the present sovereign have been crowned. To speak more exactly, however, they have crowned themselves; for no one is deemed worthy at that solemn hour to place upon the Emperor's brow the emblem of sovereignty save the Czar himself. There we beheld the very platform upon which they have all in succession stood.

Four gigantic gilded and pictured columns support the five great domes, and the most sacred pictures of Russia line the walls from pavement to cupola like a sacred tapestry of gold. Let me mention one of these pictures. It is a portrait of the Virgin Mary, supposed to have been painted by St. Luke. On one occasion it is said to have scared away the Tartars, but I do not believe the Tartars were so good judges of paintings. At all events, this picture is surrounded by a golden frame, incrusted with jewels to the value of $225,000. One emerald alone is worth $50,000. Yet how can I give you an idea of the treasures contained in the whole church? At the time of the French invasion, although all the more precious articles had been carried away by the Russians, the soldiers of Napoleon obtained here no less than five tons of silver and five hundred pounds of gold. Upon the sacred altar of this church I saw an imitation of Mt. Sinai, made of pure gold. There, too, is a Bible covered with precious jewels, a present from the mother of Peter the Great. This is probably the largest Bible in the world. At all events it ought to be, for it requires two men to carry it, weighing as it does more than one hundred pounds. Furthermore, there are shown here, enclosed in costly caskets, a part of Christ's robe, a drop of John the Baptist's blood, a nail of the true cross, the skull of St. John, the dried tongue of Peter, and many other relics, precious to those who believe in them, and disgusting to those who do not.

One interesting thing I had almost forgotten. Whenever the Czar visits Moscow, he is driven directly through the Redeemer Gate to this cathedral. Entering, he approaches a silver casket which contains the body of St. Philip, a former bishop of Moscow. Through a small hole in the coffin-lid the withered forehead of this dead prelate is exposed to view, and upon this the Czar of all the Russias reverently places his lips. And why? Because this bishop, having dared more than three hundred years ago to reprove Ivan the Terrible for his brutal cruelty, was dragged from the altar of this cathedral, driven through the streets with brooms, and put to death. He is therefore justly regarded as a martyr, and his tomb has become a sacred shrine. Sincerely or not, therefore, the Czar deems it advisable to honor the murdered prelate. But it is easier to kiss a dead bishop than to be reproved by a living one.

Closely adjoining this historic church is the magnificent palace of the Czars. This structure, beautiful though it be, presents by its modern appearance (for most of it is only thirty years old) a startling contrast to the other buildings of the Kremlin, on which the hand of Time seems to have rested heavily.

Between the ancient and the modern portions of this building stands the antique chapel of the Czars, whose gilded domes have reflected the sun for many centuries. This contains an image of the Virgin before which, according to the priests, all must bow, or incur the risk of eternal damnation. In the old times, when the patriarchs of the church were almost equal in power to the Emperor, it was the custom, after the installation of one of these prelates, for the bishop to mount a donkey at the door of this church, and ride through the city, while the Czar himself in humility walked before, holding the bridle like a groom! Leading up to this, and also to the old palace, we note with interest a flight of steps called the "Red Staircase." It is here that the Czar shows himself to the people after his coronation in the Cathedral of the Assumption. This is to Moscow what the "Giants' Staircase" is to Venice. Horrible scenes of cruelty and bloody vengeance have been perpetrated on its ruddy steps by Ivan

KREMLIN PALACE.

the Terrible, and other despotic Czars; such as when Ivan, enraged at a letter brought him by an innocent messenger, drove his iron-pointed staff directly through the poor man's foot into the topmost stair, and then leaned on it while he re-read the letter; the wretched messenger meantime remaining motionless, not daring even to groan! Yet this is nothing to some other deeds enacted on these steps, of whose horrors I will spare you the description. Let me only add, that it was by this staircase too that Napoleon, followed by his marshals, ascended to take possession of the palace of the Kremlin.

The Muscovite home of the Russian Sovereign is in some respects superior even to the great Winter Palace of St. Petersburg, and is one of the most richly adorned structures in the world. The material of its exterior is not altogether such as we could wish, but we have ceased to be surprised at this in Russian architecture, and observe with satisfaction that at least its creamy color is still fresh and beautiful. But it is when we pass within this Imperial abode that we realize its regal splendor, especially as we enter the famous Hall of St. George. The figure of this saint mounted on a white horse forms now a part of the arms of the Russian Empire, as well as of the city of Moscow. Moreover, St. George has long been popular in Russia, owing to the power which he is supposed to wield over wolves and serpents, and the Russian peasant will never turn his cattle out to graze before St. George's day, the 23d of April, when he fancies he can do so with security! This magnificent hall is two hundred feet long, and its elaborately ornamented ceiling arches fifty-eight feet above the pol-

ST. GEORGE'S HALL.

ished marble floor.   To add to the brilliancy of the scene, the names
of individuals and regiments decorated with the order of St. George

ST. ANDREW'S HALL.

(the highest military order in the land) are inscribed on the walls in
letters of gold; the capitals of the columns are surmounted by statues of Victory bearing shields; and the gorgeous chandeliers hold
no less than three thousand two hundred candles, which, when
lighted, flood the grand apartment with a radiance rivalling that of
day.

At right angles with the Hall of St. George, is another magnificent
apartment, the Hall of St. Andrew.   Although we see a mere section

of this, in reality it is even larger than the hall which we have left. Twisted pillars, enriched by flowers of gold, rise on all sides, while fourteen lofty mirrors reflect as many windows, opening out on the balconies of the Kremlin.   The inlaid floor is wonderfully designed; every kind of colored wood being used to produce most intricate patterns of scroll and flower.   Its walls are hung in light pink silk and gold, and it is lighted by four thousand five hundred candles. Its gorgeous ceiling, sparkling with gilding and heraldic devices, glitters sixty-eight feet above us, while the wall which we are facing forms a beautiful expanse of marble, golden ornamentation, and paintings.   On the right and left of the doorway, are two black velvet stands, on which are placed the gold and silver plate of the Imperial family, when the Czar is residing here.

Passing between these, and beneath the richly decorated portal, we found ourselves before the throne of the Czar.   It is a seat worthy of an Imperial potentate.   Marble steps lead up to its lofty canopy, which fairly blazes with gold and jewels, and is surmounted by a glittering crown; the whole being relieved against a wall lined with light blue silk.   Within we see the richly gilded chair itself, behind which is a background of purple velvet, embroidered with jewels, gold insignia, and the double-headed eagle of the empire. Looking at it, we shudder at the thought of the power which its occupant possesses.   For from this throne his sceptre extends over one hundred millions of Jews, Christians, Mohammedans, Buddhists and Pagans; and his will is law, from the Chinese wall to the German frontier, and from the Polar Sea to Mt. Ararat and the Indus!

Moreover, would you know how this Czar is popularly represented to his people?   In the catechism taught them by their priests, the Czar is addressed as "our God on earth," and his "worship" is commanded on penalty of eternal torture in the future life.   To disobey his commands or the mandates of his minions is declared to be impiety against God.

I have in my possession the translation of a sermon recently preached by the metropolitan bishop of Moscow, the highest eccle-

THE THRONE OF THE CZAR.

siastic in this the holiest city of the Russian Empire. In this discourse occur the following words: "We believe that our most pious Sovereign is inspired by the Holy Spirit of God in every act, for the good of his people! He is the anointed one through whom God himself governs us! He makes laws for us, and we receive them as the gift of God! His will decides our lot, and we submit to it without a murmur; for it is the will of God!"

Is this the nineteenth century, when the head of the Greek

church in Moscow can thus proclaim the infallibility and inspiration of Alexander II. ?   But there is something even more astonishing than this.   For in another place he says : "We believe also that all the officials appointed over us by the Czar are likewise guided and inspired by God in all their decisions and acts."   Think of that ! Russian officials, the most corrupt and unprincipled body of men to be found in any government on earth, detested and hated by all intelligent Russians, even by those who have no sympathy with Nihilists and who love and pity their Czar, — Russian officials, including the monsters of cruelty in the secret police, the greatest cause of Russia's oppression and misery, — these men, whose infamous reign of corruption and tyranny must and will be broken, *these* are said by the bishop to be guided and inspired by the Divine

A STAIRCASE IN THE KREMLIN.

Spirit! What wonder that the Government ordered one hundred and twenty thousand copies of that sermon printed and distributed among the people? Ah! what a reward that bishop must have received!

As I was ascending one of the magnificent stairways of this palace, my friend recalled to me a story which we had read in the "Revue de Deux Mondes," which gives an illustration of these "infallible" Czars strangely at variance with the idea of divine inspiration. Many years ago, this palace was one night resounding with the merriment of a public ball. During those hours of gayety, the Czar, Paul I., noticed a young officer, named Labanoff, paying special attention to a young French actress of whom he was madly jealous. He at once ordered Labanoff to be arrested and thrown into prison. Doubtless he only intended to keep him there a few days, but somehow (very strangely for an inspired sovereign) he forgot him! More than fifty years after, Alexander I. ascended the throne, and in clemency ordered the prisoners in a certain dungeon to be released.

In one subterranean cell, so small that it was impossible there for any one to stand erect, was found an old white-haired man, bent almost double and unable to speak intelligibly. This was Labanoff! All these years had passed; Czar after Czar had ascended the throne; but Labanoff was always forgotten! When taken out, he could not bear the light. He could not stand erect. Nor could he take more than two or three steps before he would automatically turn, as though his head had struck against the wall. He died a few days after his liberation. Comment on such absolute and infallible power as this is needless.

The most interesting apartments in the Kremlin palace are to be found in the ancient portion of the building. For there we seem to enter into the real Russian life of the old Czars, and are continually reminded of the time when Moscow was the great centre of the empire rather than St. Petersburg. One of the most remarkable of these apartments is the old banqueting-room of the Russian sovereigns. Around a column in the centre the Imperial plate is always displayed on the occasion of a royal feast; and here, after his coronation in the neighboring cathedral, the Czar, adorned for the first time with all the Imperial insignia, dines with his nobles, — not

at the same table, however, for with him only crowned heads are allowed to sit. On the wall also is a little balcony, which, during the coronation banquet, is occupied by the members of the Imperial family; for even their presence at the Emperor's table is then excluded by etiquette.

Another room of great historic interest in this wing of the palace is the ancient bedroom of the Czars. There was to

THE BANQUET HALL.

me a horrible fascination in looking on this antique couch and thinking of the men who once had slept beneath that canopy. For the history of the Czars of that time is the most horrible and revolting that I know of. Indeed, compared to Ivan the Terrible, Tiberius, Caligula, and Nero seem innocent and peaceable. It would be hard to find another such record of atrocities as his on any page of history. It was during his reign that the famous Russian proverb was invented, "Near to the Czar, near to death!"

It was he, you remember, who utterly destroyed one of his own cities, Novgorod, containing four hundred thousand inhabitants. Having been enraged at it, his orders to his soldiers were, "Burn, slay, and give no quarter to old or young." In consequence, the streets were filled with blood, and sixty thousand persons were slaughtered. This Ivan would walk about the streets of Moscow ordering this one or that to be killed. One day at dinner he killed one of his sons, with a blow from his iron staff. At another time he had five hundred of his nobles tortured and thrown into caldrons of boiling water.

One day as he was passing through this palace, the idea seized him to have his little hump-backed jester sprinkled with boiling soup. As the poor creature did not laugh at this joke, he killed him

THE ANCIENT BEDROOM OF THE CZARS.

with a blow of his knife. Then he turned and cut off the ear of one of his courtiers. This man very wisely thanked him for leaving him the other, and thus saved his head. One instance more, and I will mention no more of his atrocities. He was fiendish enough to punish some of his nobles by hanging their wives and leaving them suspended over the doors of their homes for days, so that they must push aside their corpses to go in and out! And yet this man pretended that God was acting through him in these deeds; and actually, after some of his most horrible crimes, he would say to his quaking subjects: "I ask an interest in your prayers!" In view of these and countless other facts connected with Ivan's reign of fifty years, I was startled to read in the Hermitage at St. Petersburg the following autograph letter of the Czar Nicholas, father of the late Alexander: "The Czar Ivan the Fourth was severe and violent, which gave him the name of 'the Terrible.' He was however just, brave and generous, and contributed to the happiness and development of his country!" Signed, "Nicholas."

It may be that this throws some new light upon the character of Ivan; but it likewise explains something of the tyranny of the reign of Nicholas.

The right wing of this palace is called the Treasury, and contains such a marvellous collection of historic relics and magnificent souvenirs of conquest, that it would be folly for me to attempt to describe them in detail. Here are preserved the coronation dresses of many of the Empresses, and the jewels and insignia of former Czars. From its connection with Asia, Persia, and India, Russia has always had unusual opportunities to secure a multitude of precious objects; and certainly, with the exception of the Sultan's Treasury at Constantinople, I have never seen such a display as this.

As we walk along, we see at every turn crowns flashing with resplendent colors, and sceptres radiating waves of brilliancy. If you deem this extravagant, remember that one of these sceptres alone contains no less than two hundred and sixty-eight diamonds and three hundred and sixty rubies! A throne from Persia is there, still blazing with three thousand precious stones; and here, under a protecting canopy of velvet and gold and surrounded by jewels, we see the double throne upon which sat together, as sovereigns of Russia, those two brothers one of whom was destined soon to rule alone under the well-earned title of Peter the Great.

Here also we observe with interest the elegant canopy, under

THE TREASURY.

which the Czar walks in solemn procession to and from his coronation.

Here, too, is a chair containing, it is said, a piece of the true cross; and here, in striking contrast to all this dazzling wealth, I beheld the simple camp bedstead, once occupied by Napoleon, and captured by the Russians during the fearful retreat of the French across the Beresina.

Naturally enough, on leaving the Kremlin, which is at once the

THE CHURCH OF ST. BASIL.

fortress and the altar of this city of the Czar, we paid a visit to the neighboring church of St. Basil, the most magnificent of ancient Russian shrines.

The appearance of this extraordinary structure is familiar to every traveller, long before he actually beholds it, for it is always represented in pictures as a characteristic monument of Moscow, and adorns nearly every illustrated geography. As we survey this edifice, so unlike any other in the world, we naturally ask, "Who was this St. Basil who has been thus immortalized?" He was, it seems, a popular prophet and miracle-worker three centuries ago. This was not all, however. He claimed, as his distinctive glory, that he was "idiotic for Christ's sake," whatever that may mean! Ivan the Terrible erected this structure over the grave of Basil the Imbecile; and in it were also placed the relics of another weak-headed saint, called "John the Idiot." In plain English, therefore, this celebrated church was erected by the Russian Nero over the graves of two idiots! I assure you, I am not jesting. Idiocy is a form of religious mendicancy very common in Russia, and imbeciles are treated with great consideration. Beggars in Moscow even now feign idiocy, and go barefooted in winter about the city. But very few of these are saints. In the crypt of this church are kept the heavy chains and crosses which St. Basil wore for penance, and the iron weights worn by the other idiot. Basil's cap was carried off by the French in 1812, and the inestimable treasure has never been recovered.

As for the edifice itself, it is a wonderful specimen of Byzantine architecture and is unlike anything else in the world. Nor is this strange. When it was finished, Ivan the Terrible found it so beautiful and remarkable, that he called before him the architect and asked him if he could ever build another such temple. The artist, hoping doubtless for a fresh opportunity to display his skill, proudly answered, "Yes." "That, by Heaven, you shall never do," cried Ivan, and caused his head to be immediately cut off, in order that this church might forever remain without a rival. Can you imagine a jealousy more cruel and at the same time more flattering than this? The style of St. Basil's is in the highest degree incoherent and amazing, yet in a certain sense beautiful. From the roof rise eleven towers of beautiful form, each having a different design, and crowned by cupolas resembling the turbans of Oriental giants. Beneath each of these, within, is a tiny chapel, from which we looked up into the roof, as from the bottom of a well, only to find in the ceiling a huge mosaic eye, startling us by the vivid scrutiny with which it seemed to regard us. But that which is its especial glory, and causes it to seem like a glittering mirage, or a mountain in fairyland, is the fact that the whole cathedral glows, from its base to the summit of its bulbous domes, with the greatest variety of colors, which nevertheless harmonize admirably and produce an astonishing effect. Red, blue, green, yellow, white and purple, all of these are strangely blended here in one picturesque mass, like a castle made of prisms.

I admit that it is strange, fantastic, and to many even displeasing from its very oddity; but to me it seemed precisely suited to the half-barbaric Muscovite capital, and I surveyed it always with a singular feeling of satisfaction.

And if I thus admired it in summer, how beautiful must it appear in the winter time! For then the golden rays of the sun not only gleam upon its wealth of colors, but likewise sparkle on these towers with their silver frosting, the windows with their diamond pendants, and all its countless ornaments and crosses, set in a mass of glittering crystals, cut by the unrivalled lapidaries of the frosty air.

It was by moonlight on a summer evening that we went forth from our hotel, and standing near St. Basil's church took a farewell look at the Kremlin. Never before had Moscow seemed to me such an Oriental city; for its gilded towers sparkling in the moonbeams recalled the Turkish minarets which I had often watched thus from the Bosphorus. I thought then of the night which Napoleon passed within those Kremlin walls — apparently a conqueror, but really on the verge of a sublime catastrophe! "We shall see," he had exclaimed on entering the Kremlin, "what the Russians will do. If they refuse to treat with me, our winter-quarters are assured. We shall give to the world the singular spectacle of an army wintering in an enemy's country. In the springtime will come mild weather and — victory!" Napoleon believed that his genius had foreseen everything. It had indeed foreseen every possibility, save one, —namely, the suicide of Moscow!

As the exultant French entered the city which seemed to them the goal of their desires, they found it a desert without food or inhabitants. Even here the Russian army persisted in its policy of retreating and never fighting; for well it knew that in the field the Eagles of France moved only to victory.

Its population of three hundred thousand had fled, and only

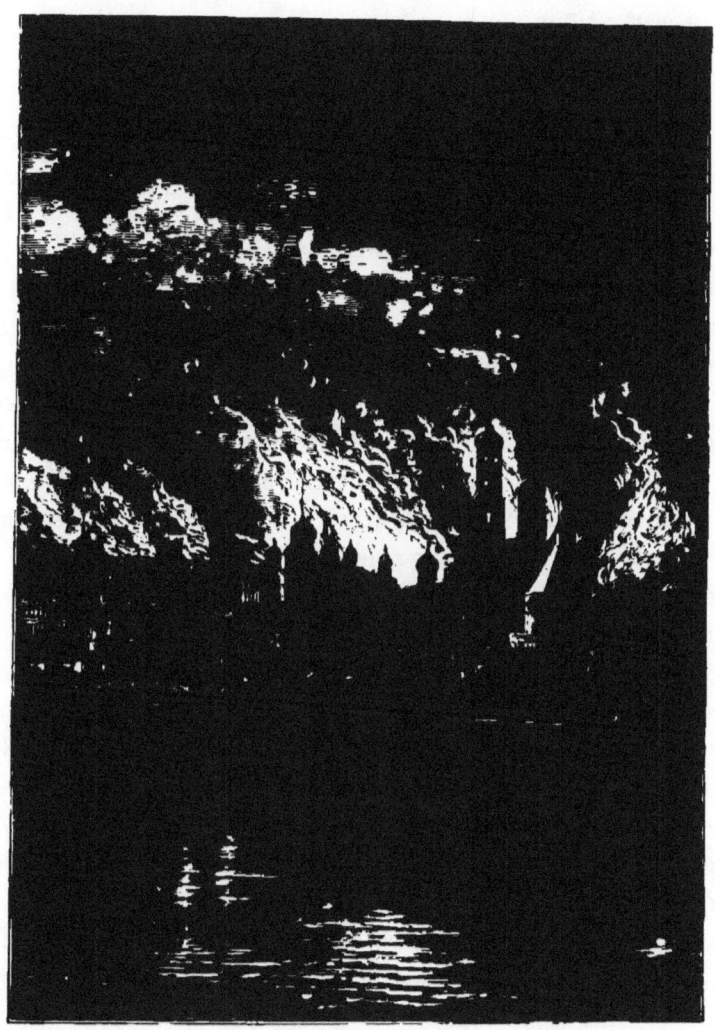

THE SUICIDE OF MOSCOW.

some liberated convicts and abandoned wretches watched the triumphant entry of the conqueror. It was appalling. The French were starving, and Moscow was empty! But this was only the commencement.

Scarcely had Napoleon entered the Kremlin, when the liberated

convicts began their work, and those flames burst forth whose lurid
after-glow was to light the path to Waterloo and St. Helena!

There was something sublime in this act of the Russians. To
thwart the otherwise invincible Napoleon, they gave up to the devouring element their ancient, beautiful and holy city, although it was
the idol of every Russian heart, and though her shrines were to him
the holiest in the world, hallowed by seven centuries of historical
association! This fearful sea of flame spoke, therefore, in a million
fiery tongues of the grandest sacrifice ever made to national feeling.

Starting from eleven different places, the conflagration raged for
three days with terrific fierceness. The Russians had removed all
the engines, and the dismayed French could do almost nothing to
check it, though the incendiaries were shot down like dogs. But
what words can describe the horror of that scene? Amid the glorious palaces and churches resplendent in the flames, the convicts
and abandoned wretches ran like vermin, engaged in universal pil-
lage, and covering their filthy rags with furs and gems and costly
robes. What the fire spared, the greedy clutch of ravishers destroyed; and works of elegance and luxury went down either in
the awful holocaust or in the vortex of remorseless war. No less
than twenty thousand Russian soldiers who had been left in the
Moscow hospitals were burned to death.

What wonder that Napoleon, though quartered in the Kremlin,
now sought to make peace with his peculiar foe? But now the
Russians laughed, and Kutusoff, their leader, answered: "I have
but just opened the campaign, for now I see approaching my ally,
WINTER!" And then commenced that terrible retreat whose horrors have baffled the power of brush and pencil to portray. All the
annals of war furnish no parallel to the story of that march, which
has been forever frozen into the memory of man. The frost and
snow made frightful havoc with the host which in the most awful
scenes of carnage had never blanched. Such was their agony for
food that officers and soldiers alike fought for the carcasses of the
horses as they fell, and ate them raw.

Freezing, yet struggling to the last against the eddying snow and piercing wind, they staggered on, till one after another fell from the ranks, to be coffined only in the shroud of ice woven around them by the pitiless storm-king. The exact extent of the French loss is unknown, but a Russian account states that when the icy mantle of the Beresina had melted in the spring, there were found in the river alone thirty-six thousand dead bodies! They were the last ghastly remnant of the one hundred and thirty thousand who perished on that fearful march, from cold, hunger and fatigue!

NAPOLEON.

"Turn back, turn back, thou fur-clad Emperor,
   Thus toward the palace of the Tuileries
   Flying with breathless speed. Yon meagre forms,
Yon breathing skeletons, with tattered robes,
And bare and bleeding feet, and matted locks,
Are these the high and haughty troops of France,
The buoyant conscripts, who from their blest homes
Went gayly at thy bidding? When the cry
Of weeping Love demands her cherished ones,
The nursed upon her breast, — the idol-gods
Of her deep worship, — wilt thou coldly point
   The Beresina, the drear hospital,
The frequent snow-mound on the unsheltered march,
   Where the lost soldier sleeps?"

I know not how it is with other visitors to Moscow, but for me there was a spectre in this Kremlin! A face there was that gazed on me from every wall and waited silently for me at every gate! A sad and troubled face, whose classic features seemed cut in marble, so livid was their pallor, and in whose eyes there shone a momentary gleam of fear, as though their penetrating glance had already caught the coming obscuration of his star of destiny. It was the face of Napoleon, vanquished by the unconquerable North, and turning from the flames of Moscow to commence that downward path which ended only in the lonely grave at St. Helena. As I left the Kremlin, the bells in the Ivan tower were sounding, as though they were tolling Napoleon's funeral knell!

University Press: John Wilson & Son, Cambridge.